SCOTT HARDIE

TROPHY OF GOD'S GRACE

THE RESTORATION OF A MARRIAGE

TROPHY OF GOD'S GRACE

Unless otherwise specified, all Scripture quotations are taken from the NIV® Bible (The Holy Bible, New International Version®), copyright © 1973, 1978, 1984, 2011 by Biblica, Inc.® Used by permission of Biblica, Inc.® All rights reserved worldwide.

ISBN 978-1-6985-7227-7

Thank you...
Rebecca Hardie, Shannon Akin, Emily Edwards, Katrina Elsea, Larry Turrentine, Rick Weintraub

Cover Design: Scott Hardie

Printed in the United States of America

First Edition 2019

for Rebecca, Drew, Jake and Alex

PROLOGUE

"My marriage is over and it's all my fault." He and I were sitting in my car in the parking lot of a hotel. He was sobbing uncontrollably, his chest heaving, blurting out the words. I was stunned. What in the world? I said to myself. I had known them for more than 15 years. Had walked through their difficulty in getting pregnant. Had prayed with them. Had been there when they adopted a baby boy. Then had shared with them the joy of not one but two pregnancies. They were now a family of five with three boys. What was going on?

He calmed down and proceeded to relate the most sordid details of their marriage. How could this be? I again asked myself silently. These two were leaders in a Bible study group which I taught. She was my hairdresser and also took care of several members of my family. He was a natural leader, a talented graphic artist with his own thriving business. Sure, they had been through a tough time when their house flooded, but they seemed to have made it out of that situation. My wife and I had been to that house for birthday parties. They appeared to be a happily married couple.

Scott, with his wife Rebecca's encouragement, has set all this down in writing for one purpose: to demonstrate how an outwardly happy married couple descended into the darkness of sin, nearly destroyed their marriage and family and, with God's Presence, experienced repentance, redemption, restoration and forgiveness. It's not an easy first half to read, yet it is instructive and real-world. We human beings are susceptible to the lowest behaviors imaginable while we keep it secret from everyone around us. We can destroy relationships, hurt even those we love dearly (especially our children), all the while justifying ourselves. As you read Scott's narrative, put yourself in the picture— not necessarily that you are engaged in similar activities, but in whatever is poisoning your relationship.

The second half of Scott's heartfelt story is a template of how to experience the repentance, redemption, restoration and forgiveness that lead to a healthy relationship and a truly fulfilling marriage. Take notes, open yourself to the unvarnished truth. God tells us he has a plan for us. Stick with me, He says, and I'll show you stuff you never dreamed could be [JEREMIAH 33:3].

Scott and Rebecca are in a much better place today because they were both willing to face up to the truth and do what was required, individually and together, to heal themselves and their family. Many who read this book will be able to place themselves in the narrative. Will you be willing to heal yourselves spiritually, emotionally and physically? You're in a good place to start.

—Rick Weintraub

...PART ONE...
THIS OLD HOUSE

I didn't start drinking until I was 35 years old. My dad was an alcoholic and, from a very young age, I had sworn off alcohol. I had experienced how insidious addiction could be and I wanted no part of that scene. No way. No how.

It started with a glass of wine for this dinner, then a glass for that lunch. Within five years, I'd graduated to drinking enough wine to achieve a buzz before lunchtime.

Wine led to margaritas which led to mixed drinks and then straight hard liquor. Not the best drink menu for a man whose family tree included quite a few branches of men who had addiction problems.

I'd pretty much checked off every action item on the list of "WHAT NOT TO DO" if you have a family history of alcohol abuse.

But there I stood—albeit a bit wobbly—totally convinced that "I can handle it!" HashTagFamousLastWords.

I was like a house that had great curb appeal... I looked young for my age, didn't cuss, didn't drink—as far as anyone knew at the time. I was married to a beautiful bride. We enjoyed spending time with our three young sons. We were very active in our local church: co-directing couples' Bible study classes, participating in various city missions and sponsoring youth events. It all made for a very nice brochure for a home anyone would be interested in buying. But beyond the glossy exterior paint I had become infested with termites and I was crumbling from the inside out.

When I look back now, I realize that alcohol was a gateway drug for me. It wasn't the typical gateway to illicit drug use. Nope. For me it was a gateway to illicit sexual behavior.

In the same way that rotten wood invites parasites and the destruction they inflict on the interior of a building, my uninhibited use of alcohol became the perfect breeding ground for sexual immorality to take root and grow unabated within the four walls of my "perfect" life. Once the infestation was complete our seemingly idyllic home was literally torn apart at the seams by the crushing weight of spiritual warfare fueled by outright personal rebellion.

This is a story that gets seedy. That's one of the reasons it has taken so long to write. I've wrestled with the balance of sharing enough of the details to be transparent while steering clear of putting thoughts and images into people's minds that don't really need to be there. As we forge ahead please bear with me. I want you to know that when it seems like I'm glossing over a moment or detail it's meant as protection, not deflection.

The purpose of this book is to glorify God—the God of the universe who stepped into the middle of a tragedy and rewrote it into an epic love story full of grace, redemption and hope.

With that being said, let me place my hard hat securely in place, pull on my heavy duty work gloves, take my tools in hand—essentially my thumbs and iPhone keyboard—and start building the framework of a story I like to call, "Trophy of God's Grace."

PAINTING W/O THE NUMBERS

We all have that one light switch in our home. You know the one. No matter how many times you tug up and down on it, nothing seems to happen! The one right next to it seems to control the overhead light fixture but that one switch simply remains an enigma.

You've set it to the "on" position and circled your entire property to see if something has been illuminated, but alas—nothing! Common sense tells you that once the switch is flipped, the current should open, the electricity should flow, and a light should come on somewhere. But with this one mystery switch it's a no-go! Even though it looks usable there is just no power there. It simply leaves you in the dark.

When I flipped the switch on my sexuality, I was hoping for the electricity that can come from dabbling in the unknown and taboo.

All I experienced was darkness: a lurid murkiness that swept over my mind, my heart, and eventually my entire home.

It would be easy to say that our lives went from "awesome" to "gruesome" in the time it takes to flip a light switch, that hanging out in X-rated chat rooms and lying down with prostitutes just kinda happened on the spur of the moment. Oops. My bad. Just a moment of indiscretion. But that's wishful thinking. It took years of effort to pull down the switch and when we finally got it, boy did it get dark—like Vantablack dark! No. That's not a new Harry Potter villain. It's a paint. Have you ever seen it? It's crazy! You should Google it right now and check it out! Surrey NanoSystems, the UK company that developed it in 2014, touts it as "the world's blackest black." They've created a non-reflective substance that absorbs 99.6% of the light that hits it. It's so dark that it makes 3D objects look flat! [Resource: https://mymodernmet.com/vantablack-worlds-blackest-black/]

While it took Surrey several years of experimentation to succeed, it took us quite a few years of marriage to fail. You know, it's hard enough to admit this all went down in the first place; but it's super painful to realize that, in many regards, we'd set ourselves up for failure from the very beginning.

8.8.92. I love those numbers! They mean so much to me! It's the day Rebecca and I were married. It was a glorious day!

I'll never forget the smile she had on her face and how she was simply glowing with beauty! How bright the light of the sun was dancing through her hair and intermingling with her veil. The rays were streaming over her like the brush strokes of a virtuoso painter. It was like someone was creating their grand masterpiece right in front of my eyes!

I'll never forget how long it took Grandpa Kurtz to shuffle over to join the guests seated on either side of the pitcher's mound in white chairs strategically placed in the infield. The VHS tape of his epic journey is classic viewing in our home.

I'll never forget how the limo pulled through the left field gate, parked behind second base, how Rebecca and her dad walked down the strip of green indoor/outdoor carpet and, after a little misstep traversing the pitching rubber, joined me, her mom, her best friend, my dad, my best friend and our Music Minister at home plate!

Yep. You're reading all that right. We were married on a softball field in August in Texas in the middle of the day. Uhm... maybe it wasn't a totally sound idea [i.e. the 100-degree heat being an issue] but it worked for us!

At the time, I worked at a Cancer Treatment Center as a X-ray File Room Technician—a fancy name for someone who had the capacity to file large manila folders full of film in in alphabetical order in a book shelf and then later find them and hand them to someone who needed them. I was obviously highly trained and apparently highly gullible as I was talked into being the head coach for our company's co-ed softball team.

As the head coach it was my job to build the roster for every game. Our team had to have at least 5 guys and 5 girls in the lineup, and it was a weekly struggle to find enough girls to play. During one such week of desperation, I was racking my brain trying to think of a worthy female candidate. I thought of Rebecca Kime. She was tall, athletic, personable—and my roommate's ex-girlfriend. No drama here, folks. They were a year removed from being an item. I knew she played softball and I knew she would be an easy-going, fun person to be around. I got her number, called her, asked her to play, and the rest is history!

She played the first week and again the next week, after which I asked her out on a date. Two weeks later we were sitting at Ryan's buffet restaurant— spare no expense. You do remember the job title, right? While we were eating God knows what, we found ourselves talking about wedding colors and venues. We both conceded that the super nice churches in town were kind of expensive to rent so, half-joking, I offered, "Why don't we get married on the softball field? It's $15 an hour to rent." I could see the light bulb go on over Rebecca's head!

Eight months after that there we stood face-to-face in the dirt on the Green Field basically where our relationship had begun...

I'll never forget how excited I was, how happy I was and how SCARED I was!

I had NO idea what I was getting into! I loved her and I was convinced that I was ready to spend my life with her. But, honestly, I didn't really understand the magnitude of what I was doing; of how important this covenant was to God; of how truly unprepared I was to take on the task set before me. EPHESIANS 5:25-27 puts it quite succinctly:

"Husbands, love your wives, just as Christ loved the church and gave himself up for her to make her holy, cleansing her by the washing with water through the word, and to present her to himself as a radiant church, without stain or wrinkle or any other blemish, but holy and blameless."

Hmmm. No biggie. I got this! Okay. Not really. Even when I read it now, I'm like "Whoa." That's a doozy of a job description; a calling of the highest order! Believe me, as I looked into the beautiful blue eyes of my dream girl and my party-in-the-back mullet dripped sweat onto the collar of my shimmering silver tux, I had every intention of being that kind of husband. It was my standard. It was the target I was shooting for. Unfortunately, I would learn soon enough—and often enough—that my aim would not always be true.

It's accurate to say that the Lord's ways are not our own ways, and it's equally accurate to say the groom's ways are not the bride's ways. Within just a couple of weeks after our wedding, Rebecca and I discovered this in a somewhat dramatic fashion.

I come from a family with five siblings—four brothers and one sister—while Rebecca comes from a family with just one brother. This means that life in each of our households growing up was quite different. Those differences included how mealtime was handled and ultimately how leftovers were secured. Let's take, for instance, pizza delivery, consumption and preservation.

You see, in a family with four boys, a few large pizzas ordered for dinner would invariably never see the light of the next day. So, to keep the process simple and accessible we would put our left-over pizza boxes in the oven. Within those comfy confines, it would all stay warm and each of us could take turns grabbing a slice here or there until it was gone. It was just standard operating procedure in the Hardie household.

Conversely, in the Kime household, with only two kids and much less of a need for constant caloric intake, the pizza was bagged, tagged and placed neatly into the fridge. It might take up to a week to whittle away at the remainder. Clean, efficient, logical: the quintessential Kime way.

It was with these divergent leftover world views that Rebecca and I entered our new home together. Neither of us had even the slightest inclination that we needed to formally discuss this matter with each other. That is, until one fateful night...

We had eaten as much delivery pizza as we could, so I boxed up the remains and placed them in the oven for safekeeping, in strict accordance with Hardie tradition. The next afternoon Rebecca turned on the oven to prep for dinner. It wasn't long before there was a strange odor permeating our tiny one-bedroom apartment. Rebecca looked at me quizzically and asked, "Do you smell something burning?"

She got up from the couch, stepped into the kitchen just a few feet away and... What transpired next comes back to me in classic action movie slo-mo... As she placed her hand on the oven handle a startling realization came to me... I sprang to my feet like Ethan Hunt jumping from one building to the next, my face contorted, perspiration immediately lathered up on my forehead, my eyes bulged, and I let out a muffled, elongated "NOOOOOOOOO"...

Her grip tightened on the flimsy black plastic as the tension mounted... Time stood still for a moment... Then the door came down and a giant ball of flame burst out from behind it... Cut to black.

Her eyes darted back and forth, and her body undulated with rapid breathing... She sat on the couch, staring straight ahead... Physically she was fine; mentally the shock was just subsiding... "Why..." As I placed one hand over hers and wiped her brow with my other... "Why. Why. Why was that box in the oven?!?!" She glanced over at me as if an alien had just materialized right next to her... I looked sheepishly toward the kitchen and started to explain... "Well, you see..."

I know, kind of a silly story—but it illustrates a significant facet of marriage. The bride and groom enter into a brand-new covenant relationship with different opinions, different priorities and different personal baggage.

No matter how solid your foundation might be, if you don't understand the need to proactively navigate these differences together then the underpinnings of your relationship will slowly start to show wear and tear. A shift will occur like the adjustment of a house built on hot, dry, cracked Texas soil. You won't realize there's a problem until doors start to stick and walls start to show stress. By then you will already have a massive structural problem on your hands.

Back in the day, I loved those Paint-by-the-Numbers Kits! They were these intricate black and white etchings of, say, Yoda or Captain America or perhaps a beautiful butterfly that came with a colorful set of markers. In each white space of the drawings there would be a number that correlated with a colored marker. Find the number, match the marker, fill in the space with the appropriate color, rinse and repeat. Eventually you would end up with a fully realized image suitable for hanging in a prominent location on your bedroom wall. [Nowadays my kids do the same thing with their thumbs on their smart phone apps. I prefer to think of my way as infinitely more artsy and sophisticated.]

When I entered into marriage it felt as if I had this massive black and white etching of a relationship smack dab in front of me and I was tasked with filling it in completely. I had my relational markers out and ready to go, but no matter how hard I looked I couldn't find the numbers that would help me color in the empty spaces correctly 100% of the time.

There's no doubt that I put the wrong color here and the wrong color there. I was trying to paint without the numbers, and, over time, it was gradually getting messy. Unfortunately, I never took the time to step back and see what was really being created as a good artist should do. I wish I had squinted my eyes and looked deeper into the picture to see how the colors were reacting with each other, what was really working and what wasn't; making the adjustments as needed; starting over with a fresh canvas if need be.

I wasn't as introspective as I should've been because I was simply afraid of conflict. Growing up in my family, as I'm sure it goes for many alcoholic families, we denied the scope of the turmoil we were living in. Even though the lingering effects of my dad's disease infected every part of our lives, we didn't ever fully acknowledge it. We didn't square up and face it head on. We were under the delusion that if we didn't talk about it then it maybe, just maybe, it wasn't there.

For me, and as it turns out for Rebecca, if there wasn't any outward conflict then there wasn't really any inward problem to fix. The art of denial gave us a false sense of peace on the outside when all the while a storm was brewing on the inside. We avoided conflict and, ultimately, conflict resolution. It essentially came down to the difference between Peacekeeping and Peacemaking.

Peacekeeping focuses on surface level feelings. "How will this look to others?" If something ugly happens it is quickly tucked away behind a locked door so no one can see it. All seems fine until all the nooks and crannies are stuffed and there's nowhere left to hide anything. Sooner or later, the door holding all of the junk ruptures and the debris field covers the whole relationship.

On the other hand, Peacemaking focuses on the bigger picture. "How can we make it through this?" When the door stays open and nothing is trapped inside there isn't any danger of an unforeseen implosion. It may feel more painful up-front; but when all is said and done the issues are methodically dealt with, the appropriate conflict occurs, and every effort is made to get from one side of the issue to the other in a healthy, transparent way. The words of the Reverend Billy Graham ring so very true...

"Embracing conflict can be a joy when we know that irritation and frustration can lead to growth and the re-energizing of ourselves and others."

As duly certified Peacekeepers, from the very beginning of our relationship, Rebecca and I didn't embrace conflict. We saw no joy in it and certainly didn't see any growth coming from it either. We assumed that the absence of conflict meant we were "okay." The failure to address any of the nagging issues that were festering dangerously below the surface left plenty of stuff that wasn't up to code hidden behind a privacy fence constructed out of pride, neglect and apathy. Despite the story book beginning to our marriage, this inclination toward peacekeeping would not bode well for us in the long run. And speaking of running…

I'll never forget how our Music Minister yelled, "PLAY BALL!" and Rebecca and I bounded triumphantly down that indoor-outdoor carpet under a tunnel of raised softball bats [wielded by the members of my men's softball team]. I'll never forget how we jumped effortlessly into that limo, full to the brim with hope, dreams and love. I'll never forget how deep the tint was on the windows as we drove off. It was hard to see our surroundings; it was hard to think beyond the moment.

I had all the colors I needed to fill in the blank spaces to come. God's Word and Spirit were readily available to me. I could rely on Him and love on this woman with all my heart for the rest of my life! Marriage could always be just like this wonderfully mind-altering limo ride! Right?!?

I could have never fathomed that I would eventually grow weary of coloring inside the lines; that I would lose touch with the blessings that God had set before me, ready to go, within the boundaries of His holiness; that I would become so completely numbed by the daily grind of life; that I would sit alone in pure darkness.

NO ESCAPE ROOM

I'm a child of the 80's. Stone-washed jeans. Member's Only jackets. Big hair. Neon leggings. Mixtapes. MTV. Cheesy action movies. Aww yeah! John Rambo. Indiana Jones. Rocky Balboa. John McClane. These action movies all had the same basic m/o: bloodless body counts, a two-dimensional villain that you just love to hate—rocking some obligatory thick foreign accent—a smattering of over-the-top catch phrases and, the pièce de résistance, the melodramatic workout training montage! [YouTube "80s movie training montages" and you'll get the idea.]

The cookie-cutter premise goes like this: Our hero is faced with insurmountable odds; the competition is way out of his league and he's woefully low on resources. He's all out of options! What will he do?

Well, first things first, he needs to review...

The 80's Movie Training Montage Checklist:

- ✓ Discover a relatively unknown big hair band—muscle shirts; tight jackets; flipped-up collars; feathered hair; fashionable headbands optional—and make sure they have enough musical ability to craft at least one "one hit wonder" song!
- ✓ Hire a personal trainer and get ripped like nobody's business!
- ✓ Cue music, drench body with "sweat" and work out for the cameras! Once noticeable physical metamorphosis has occurred cut to the hero sitting alone—dramatically staring off into the distance—contemplating the climactic showdown to come.

Now with all of that in mind, let's picture a different type of montage. Pick out your favorite '80s band—maybe Survivor or Def Leppard—but instead of a celebrity workout sequence, let's splice together scenes from the Hardie family circa 1992-2010...

1992... Moving boxes... first apartment... pizza box fireball... long nights of playing "Hook" on the Nintendo 64... X-ray File Room Technician... crazy neighbors fighting next door... paper thin walls...

1993... Moving boxes... new apartment down the street... third floor stairs... hand-made foam core geometric art on the walls... first pet, Cato the iguana... previous neighbors move next door... eye roll... can't do that again...

1994... Moving boxes... tiny home... art school... RIP Cato... Shelby the sheltie... Ripken the white schnauzer... welcome to the fam... infertility... prayer, patience, impatience, anger, treatments, acceptance...

1997... Moving boxes... new subdivision... small company graphics job... synthesizers swell... adoption... jump in the car... three dresses in hand thinking it's a girl... Drew is ours... first-born son... looks like a little old man... synthesizers swell... pregnancy, shock, awe, praise... Jake makes his way... head as big as his body... diapers... financial turmoil... downsizing... finding new homes for the dogs... RadioShack graphics job...

2002... Moving boxes... rent house with pink carpet... Barney on the TV... synthesizers swell... welcome Alex to the world... full dark hair standing on end... purple lips... can't breathe... seven days in NICU... coaching Little League... out of room... need more space...

2003... Moving boxes... buyers again... tall trees and a basketball goal... corporate lay-off... freelance graphics job... home office in the bedroom... travel required... Orlando, Vegas, New York and everywhere in between... alcohol starts flowing... foundation problems with the home... cracks starting to show...

2005... Moving boxes... cul-de-sac... creek flowing... friends nearby... sleep walking kids... the clothes hamper is NOT a toilet... back porch birthday parties... hard liquor above the fridge...

porn streaming on the screen... fantasies played out... boundaries unseen... last ominous synthesizer key held down tight and released... fade to black.

April 14th, 2011... I sat up on the edge of my bed—one foot on the floor, the other tangled up in the sheets—looking off into the distance, contemplating the full life I'd lived. Couldn't sleep. The silence was too loud. Every light in my northern Miami hotel room was on but it still seemed so dark. I could sense the palm trees leaning against the wind outside, but I couldn't see them.

I was trapped in an escape room whose walls were covered in Vantablack—all the light swallowed up—leaving nothing in its place. No matter how hard I strained my eyes to see I couldn't find a way out—no doors, no windows, no escape.

I'd just finished my week-long run working as a graphics operator at a corporate event. The long day in the ballroom had concluded so I joined the A/V crew down by the pool. During the festivities, I pretty much consumed an entire bottle of Scotch. They were celebrating a job well done. I was lamenting the loss to come.

This time the liquor didn't really faze me. It offered no relief. In fact, it would be the last time I would ever drink. No matter how painful the emotions might be, I wanted to feel them. I had no desire to be numb anymore.

After a while, I said good-bye to my work friends and wandered up to my room. My heart sat so heavy in my chest it was hard to breathe. As the door latched behind me, I leaned back against it for a moment trying to keep the worries and fears from breaking in. I realized that wasn't going to work so I gathered my stuff, packed my bags and dropped into bed exhausted. Moments later, my weary eyes popped open.

There I was crumpled up on a lumpy mattress uncomfortably aware of the climactic showdown ahead of me. I was just a few hours away from boarding the longest plane ride of my life. I was going back to Texas, to what was left of home—it was the beginning of the end.

Regardless of the gloom that surrounded me, I offered up constant and fervent prayers. I knew that God was with me. I'd already felt His power in my life, already experienced the miracle of redemption He offered. I took solace in the words of HEBREWS 4:16...

"Let us then approach God's throne of grace with confidence, so that we may receive mercy and find grace to help us in our time of need."

I asked for His presence in the chaos. I asked for comfort. I asked for continued healing. I asked for His light to fill the darkness. It was hard to believe everything that had happened. It was hard to see any hope.

God created sex for us. It is good—like knock-your-socks-off good—when it is used as it was designed to be used. It is meant to be the culmination of intimacy between a man and a woman within the covenant of marriage. Paul emphasizes the point in EPHESIANS 5:31-33...

"'For this reason a man will leave his father and mother and be united to his wife, and the two will become one flesh.'" This is a profound mystery—but I am talking about Christ and the church. However, each one of you also must love his wife as he loves himself, and the wife must respect her husband.'"

One flesh. Christ and the church. Love. Respect. It sounds like so much more than just physical, doesn't it?

Within the security of the marriage covenant, the bride opens herself up to the groom, giving of herself, and in response the groom offers his strength to her. They become "one flesh." They experience the heightened pleasure of two souls baring themselves to one another. Alive. Generous. Vulnerable. Accepting.

This level of intimacy is compared to the relationship between Christ and the church. A healthy marriage based on true intimacy is such an amazing example of Christ's love—a chance for the full scope of the Gospel to influence others!

When we experience the trust and acceptance that are found in full-on "one flesh" intimacy we realize that we can truly know and be known. It's not simply a physical interaction. The physical act symbolizes the spiritual bond; wrongs can be made right; hurts can be healed; love can become real.

On the flip side, when sex is used as simply a means to an end—for the man as a physical release and for the woman as a chance at emotional validation—the effects can be disastrous. The physical simply stays physical; the spiritual tank empties; the gears of the relationship grind to a halt; love becomes a hollow fragile shell.

Honestly, I had the wrong attitude about sex. I bought into the lie that sex was just physical. I thought if I wanted it then Rebecca should want it too. And, at times, if I didn't get my way, I would grow despondent. I used my aloofness as a weapon against her. If Passive Aggressive were a people I would've most definitely been their king.

My view of sex primarily as a physical need minimized the spiritual implications of the most intimate of acts.

Sex gradually became a withdrawal from— instead of an investment in—our relationship. It became a vicious cycle of supply and demand. The more I wanted from Rebecca the less she wanted to give. As true intimacy faded, quiet indifference flourished.

I could sense Rebecca growing more distant and my response was to ramp up the sensuality. If we could really "spice things up" then we could capture a moment of pleasure that would sustain us until the next time.

My drinking and fantasies were escalating. I wasn't thinking clearly; alcohol and sex were working in tandem to desensitize me. The less I could feel the more I needed to increase the thrill. I hung out in X-rated online chat rooms; Rebecca and I watched pornographic videos together; we brought gadgets and role playing into the equation. But none of it added up to anything sustainable. With each physical act we engaged in we were tearing a hole into the center of our intimacy and dumping worthless junk into it in hopes of filling it back up.

When our lovemaking had been natural and pure—free from any extraneous elements—it had been beneficial to both of us, body, mind and soul. But we had allowed the sweetness to sour. We concocted a haphazard recipe—pouring all our wrong choices into one mess of a mixing bowl; trying in vain to regain the natural flavors we desired; trading real fruit for fake.

Sin is like a Fruit Roll-Up. Yep—that glorious brand of fruit snack that debuted in grocery stores across America in the early '80s. It's a flat, fruit-flavored snack, wrapped around a piece of cellophane for easier removal. Sounds yummy, huh? Well, at first maybe.

When you unroll the waxy coil and slap it onto your tongue it hits you with a burst of flavor. The initial explosion of sugar makes you scrabble for more! You chomp on it until it disappears, then fold up the strip into your mouth; then another fold and another.

After a while the sensation subsides, and you cram in more and more hoping to relive that first rush of flavor. The sugar turns into a slimy film covering your teeth and gums. You start to feel nauseous. What had started out as a pleasurable experience turns into quite the opposite. "Man. Wish I hadn't eaten that much!"

That's how sexual sin works. It catches your interest with a great first impression; then, after experiencing it for a while—trying to recapture that original wow factor—it just ends up making you sick.

The ingredients of a Fruit Roll-Up—straight from bettycrocker.com: Corn Syrup, Dried Corn Syrup, Sugar, Pear Puree Concentrate, Palm Oil. Contains 2% or less of: Citric Acid, Sodium Citrate, Fruit Pectin, Monoglycerides, Malic Acid, Dextrose, Vitamin C [ascorbic acid], Acetylated Monoglycerides, Natural Flavor, Color [red 40, yellows 5 & 6, blue 1].

There are lots of words in there that I can't pronounce or spell on my own. I think we can agree that this isn't quite farm-to-table natural goodness. It's a ton of processed sugar manufactured in a lab. It's fake fruit disguising itself as real. Let's compare these "fruit-flavored" snacks to actual fruit...

Apples are "composed of up to 85% water and are, therefore, excellent thirst quenchers. They contain hardly any fats or calories. Instead, they're made up of valuable ingredients such as vitamins, minerals and secondary plant substances." [southtyroleanapple.com]. Apples are full of ingredients that are natural and beneficial to our bodies.

Rebecca and I were bingeing on fake fruit. We were filling ourselves up with the empty calories of carnality, all the while craving something truly real and intimate instead. Even though our behavior was debilitating we just kept going.

I continued to demand and, in an effort to keep the peace, Rebecca continued to acquiesce. We were both violating "the sacredness of our own bodies—these bodies that were made for God-given and God-modeled love—for 'becoming one' with another" [1 CORINTHIANS 6:18 MSG].

We progressed from "harmless" role-playing between ourselves all the way to bringing a stranger into our marriage bed with us. That devastating act was far more than physical. It heightened the spiritual battle around us. It inflicted deep wounds in our innermost beings. From that point on we were struggling to tread water in an ugly cesspool. It wouldn't be long before a perfect storm would come along and drag us all the way under.

September 10th, 2010... The creek was flowing from left to right at a rapid rate. The rain was still falling like it had for days. The creek had crested to the lip of the grass but seemed to be staying there for now.

Our backyard sloped up from there to a large wooden porch. The chain link fence was swaying with the wind and the metal patio furniture glistened as the water came down from the grey sky and pelted it.

I was standing at the large bay window in our kitchen—about 75 yards from the creek—trying to gauge the urgency of the situation. As long as it was flowing, we would be okay. So far so good.

I had already moved a lot of our valuables to the garage, packed up what I could fit in my little gold Lexus coupe and dragged everything else that I could up the incline away from the driveway. Now all that was left to do was wait.

The rainfall finally ended—a small glimmer of hope. But as soon as I saw the current stop, I took a deep breath. Once it reversed its flow, I let out a deep troubled sigh. The water rose quickly. It crawled through the fence, up the hill, hopped the porch and waited patiently at our back door. "Interesting. Maybe it'll just stop there?"

My curiosity drew me to the front yard. I stepped out, turned around and faced the house. The garage was open to my right. All seemed calm for a moment. Then to my left I saw the water rushing around the corner. I backed up into the cul-de-sac as it flowed into the entry way and met the water from the back. It all converged and grew together to a height of four feet. The entire house was now submerged waist high in dark waters.

Somehow, I was still on my feet, but all of the wind was knocked out of me. I was bent over with my hands on my knees, dry heaving. A few friends from church had already showed up to help. I looked up at them and tried to talk but I could only muster a thick guttural groan.

At that instant, Rebecca pulled up in her white Yukon. She swung the door open, took a few steps toward the house, then fell to the ground screaming. I moved toward her and rested my hand on her shoulder. My head dropped as I continued to try and gather myself.

Time was running out and we had no choice but to go on the offensive. I motioned to a few of the men gathered around us and we headed toward the disaster area. We were going to salvage what we could as fast as we could.

As I waded through the water into the garage, the outdoor refrigerator was bobbing up and down like a capsized ocean freighter. I pushed it out of the way and trudged inside. I was up to my stomach in nasty water. Debris was everywhere.

Adam Sandler and Drew Barrymore were kind enough to greet me as I entered the kitchen. "The Wedding Singer" DVD floated by on its way out of the house as I took a right into the master bedroom, looking for anything above the water line that I could take to dry land.

The rescue mission lasted for about a hour. We were sorting through our stuff in the middle of the street when Drew, Jake and Alex were dropped off from school. We all embraced each other tightly and cried. We were cold, wet and homeless.

I know that not all natural disasters are a direct result of specific disobedience. Weather is just a part of living on this earth. But there's no doubt that what we experienced that day was a visual representation of the dark activities that had been going on behind the closed doors of our home for months and months.

I can see clearly now that the flood was a warning sign from God. He was trying to get us to stop what we were doing before it was too late!

The old upholstered chair creaked rhythmically as I rocked slowly back and forth. I stared down at the TV sitting on the floor in front of me. We'd salvaged it from our old game room but didn't have the chance to retrieve anything useful to set it on. I wasn't really watching it. The cadence of the chair was mesmerizing me into an almost catatonic state.

The house was a bit musty and the beds down the hall weren't very comfortable, but it was dry and functional. It was serving the purpose. We were surviving.

Our neighbor's dad had been kind enough to offer the use of his home to us. We were staying just a few blocks from the site of the flood—a site that was buzzing with activity. The structure was being rebuilt. Due to the combination of flood insurance claims and FEMA regulations we had to rebuild our old home just long enough to have it torn down.

Yay. Not too logical. But it was either that or have the entire foundation raised three feet to the tune of $60,000. We decided on the future wrecking ball option.

I'd love to tell you that the epic crisis in which we were embroiled had helped Rebecca and me grow closer; that things were getting better, and we were on the way to healing. But nothing much had really changed. My behavior certainly hadn't.

I would go out drinking at strip clubs; hanging with women I shouldn't be hanging with; thinking thoughts that I shouldn't be thinking; doing things I shouldn't be doing; all with Rebecca's knowledge and coerced consent.

Our relationship was strained at best. We went through the motions. We made it through the days and endured the nights.

Despite what I was doing on the outside, interesting things were starting to happen to me on the inside. For the first time in more than a year I was starting to feel emotions. I would even cry from time to time. Unfortunately, when the feelings got too intense, I would self-medicate with alcohol.

I was even starting to sense spiritual things again— ever so slightly. My soul was like a shortwave radio. The Holy Spirit was searching for the right frequency, trying to make contact with me. I would sense His voice every now and then. But since there was so much static crackling inside of me it came in as a scrambled signal that flickered in and out.

We would stay in this strange holding pattern for four months as the construction was completed on

what we had now affectionately dubbed "The
Storage Unit." It wasn't ever going to be our home
again. When it was finished it was just going to be a
place where our stuff resided.

December 17, 2010... With little fanfare and not
much of a reaction from Rebecca —she was
working that night—the boys and I walked back
inside our old home. "Welcome back!" We ate
pizza on a folding table in the kitchen and then went
off to bed. The whole experience was cold and
vacant; pretty much matching the look and feel of
the house itself.

We'd had it built back to its original specs. We
weren't going to put any more time and money into
it than we had to. It was a temporary situation. Once
FEMA and the city signed off on everything, we
would be out of there.

Back at our temporary housing, our boys had made
a precious green foam core Christmas tree that
stood about two and a half feet tall. It was decorated

with multi-colored pasted-on ornaments and a yellow paper star hung near the top. Now that we were "home" again, we placed it in a position of honor next to the seven-foot tree we had purchased and erected in our virtually empty living room.

Our furniture consisted of the two trees in the corner, the stockings dangling from our re-fabricated mantel and a newly acquired throw rug, a buffer between our feet and the chilly white tile floor. We circled up in camping chairs to exchange gifts on Christmas Day.

By this point, the apathy between Rebecca and I started to turn into hostility. There seemed to be even more going on behind the scenes, widening the gap between us. I sensed a weird dynamic between her and a male family friend of ours but when I mentioned it, I was rebuffed as "being all paranoid again."

And you know what? I had been so crazy over the last several months that I wasn't completely trusting my thoughts either. So, after that one heated argument in the kitchen I just let that line of questioning fall by the wayside.

Things boiled over again a couple of weeks later after Rebecca's 40th birthday party. We went out to a north Dallas restaurant with a large group of friends. There was a lot of eating, drinking and dancing. Ironically enough, I was the designated driver and didn't touch any alcohol that night.

Gradually, throughout the evening I grew very annoyed. Maybe it was because it seemed like I was the only sober person there or maybe it was the accumulated stress of the last 6 months starting to overflow. IDK. All I know is that by the time I was driving our packed SUV back home I was a time bomb ready to explode.

All it took to ignite my fuse was to miss an exit ramp and for my mother-in-law to question to me about it. I barked harshly back at her, seething in a way that was totally unnecessary. I was experiencing emotions—that was good! But the way I was expressing them—that was bad!

After that the car grew painfully quiet as Rebecca turned her head and looked out of the passenger side window. I could tell that she was holding back tears and that she was trying to get as far away from me as the door to her right would allow.

December 31, 2010... It all spilled into the next day and evening. We had driven down to San Antonio for New Year's Eve. We had a few nice moments during dinner and then afterwards at the fireworks display near the Tower of the Americas. However, in our hotel lobby, during post-fireworks cocktails, we started to argue.

Rebecca was still angry over how I had treated her mom the night before. She felt like I wasn't owning up to my behavior as completely as I should and, truth be told, I wasn't. I was being sarcastically stubborn—such a brilliant way to defuse the situation—and her reaction was to push away from me and storm toward the elevators. I left payment on the table and hurried to catch up with her. Talk about your awkward elevator ride.

We made it to our floor, and I followed her down the hallway. She swiped the keycard vigorously, entered the room and ended up near the window. I wobbled in and sat on the corner of the bed. The entire room stood empty between us.

"Are you happy?!?" She leaned her weight to one side almost stomping as she said it.

"Uh?" I started crying—like snot-rockets-shooting-out-of-the-nostrils crying.

"Are you happy?!?"

"Of course not!!" Heavy tears welled up into my eyes. It seemed like I was looking at the world through a kaleidoscope. "The last six months have sucked! The flood! Being homeless! Trying to keep it all together! It's all catching up with me!"

There was a moment where I thought she was about to tell me something more, but she stopped short. Her head lowered as she made her away across the room and sat next to me on the bed.

She put her arm over my shoulder to comfort me. I cried until it felt like my face was going to slide off onto the carpet. We held each other through the night, emotionally spent. We woke up the next morning and drove silently back up I-35 towards home.

At the time, I had no clue as to why I suffered through such a dramatic release of emotions that night. But now I realize it was more than just massive stress relief. It was the beginning of a Spirit-induced cleansing. God was laying the groundwork for something incredible and I needed to be as broken and empty as possible before I could experience it!

THE COUCH

The couch. The central hub that the rest of the home revolves around. It can have so many sizes and shapes—holding a snuggling couple or a hungry football defensive line. It can have a high back or a low back—forcing perfect posture or allowing a dramatic sprawl. It can be made out of fabric or leather—proving to be spill absorbent or spill repellent.

The couch. It has so many functions. It's where we find community—families gather to watch their favorite shows; friends come to play games and hang out. It's where we find comfort—cozy warmth when it's cold and rainy, a good conversation on a bad day.

The couch. On one day in particular it simply became an altar for me.

January 8, 2011... The morning started like so many of the mornings before. The sexual habits were already rising up inside me as had become the norm. I sat down on the couch in our living room and sank low into the leather. My spirit was heavy. I felt isolated. Without warning the memories of the past 24 months flashed through my mind like a time-lapse video.

I could see everything that had made my rebellion complete, my separation from God so profound. The selfish desires that crippled me. The sordid acts that generated so much pain. The swirling emotions that paralyzed me. It all came crashing down on me like a frigid wave from the depths of the ocean.

At first, I braced against the rush. But as the ache turned to calm, I relinquished myself to the billows rolling through my soul. Suddenly, I sensed that Jesus was sitting right next to me! I could feel His presence! I looked over and cried out to Him, "What am I doing?! Please take this away from me!"

The waters swept through all of the crevices inside me, cleaning away the dirt. I felt a jolt of electricity like a switch had been flipped. My mind, body and soul were surging with light! I enjoyed instant freedom!

"So if the Son sets you free, you will be free indeed." JOHN 8:36

What caused God to reach out and sit with me in my lowest moment? When I'd done unspeakable evil in His eyes; when I'd mocked His sacrifice with my petty thoughts; when I'd turned my back on Him. What caused God to do something so ridiculous?

LOVE.

A holy, just, perfect God is passionately in love with me. And He's passionately in love with you! Whether you just picked up your Bible ten minutes ago or ten years ago, pick it up again right now and read JOHN 3:16 with fresh eyes!

Christ has offered ALL of Himself so that He can be with you on the couch; in the hospital room; in the office cubicle; behind the locked bedroom door; anywhere and everywhere. He offers a shoulder to lean on when you're running on empty. He offers an ear to listen when no one else will. He offers to forget your wrongs if you will admit them. He offers the new in place of the old.

"Therefore, if anyone is in Christ, the new creation has come: The old has gone, the new is here!" 2 CORINTHIANS 5:17

Christ changed my life on July 13, 1983 in Arlington, Texas. The Trinity Baptist Church bus ministry picked me up from my family's apartment and whisked me off to the church's Vacation Bible School. It was there in a small back room behind the main auditorium that I heard the message of reconciliation.

A silhouette walked up to the wooden podium at the center of the space just a few feet away from me, picked up a tattered microphone and began to speak. The shadow fought through the hiccups in the audio and shared Jesus' story. When the words hit my ears, something grabbed me deep within and pulled me to the front of the room. I navigated my way through the maze of plastic classroom chairs and found someone waiting near the podium. I told them that I needed Christ.

They took me aside and explained what I'd just heard in greater detail. I listened, I understood, and I asked for forgiveness. That day, Jesus chose to extend His gift of new life to me and I chose to spend my life following Him.

Ever since then I've lived with the knowledge of my freedom, but over time I'd simply allowed myself to forget. My forgetfulness—and resulting loss of intimacy with God—had led me to desolation. His faithfulness—and refusal to let me go—had led me back to redemption.

So. There you have it. Life had changed in a BIG way for me! And... we all lived happily ever after!

Okay... Not really... Just kidding...

As a matter of fact, from this point on, it really couldn't have gotten more UN-happily ever after!

I have a weird job. I sit in dimly lit ballrooms at computers hidden behind pipe and drape. I create, edit and display pretty pictures for corporate execs. They hop on stage to convey strategy to the masses and I follow along with graphics, adding pop to the message.

The job has long hours with erratic cycles—mind-numbing stretches of standing by intermixed with extreme bouts of frantic activity. It's all quite schizophrenic really. During the down times, I'll find myself on my phone—texting, surfing, even writing a book. My conversations with Rebecca have always been a big part of my phone time.

Throughout the dog days of late 2010 and early 2011 our interactions had gotten more labored. It was not a good scene. So much was off kilter. A gigantic wall seemed to be growing higher and higher between us. It all culminated one evening in Orlando.

January 14, 2011... I'd been texting Rebecca during my break. It had been a tense back-and-forth per usual. It all felt so weird. I couldn't stand it anymore. The thought that had been swimming around in the back of my mind finally found its way to the surface. My thumbs ached as I typed and hit send.

"Is there someone else? Are you having an affair?"

My phone lit up between my hands. The glow peeked out from under the worktable and the type reflected harshly off the dark brown of my eyes. I stopped breathing. I squinted hard at the screen making sure I was seeing her answer correctly.

"We should talk about this later."

Oh my. That most definitely wasn't a "no." My heart fluttered. I looked up at my co-workers dutifully sitting at their computers on either side of me. Paula—a fiery red-headed producer with a heart of gold—leaned toward me. "Scott. You okay?"

"Uhm. I need to call Rebecca. I'll be back."

Paula glanced over at Jim on the other side of the table. Jim—a lifelong surfer and graphics guru from California—rubbed his graying goatee and offered Paula a look of concern in return. "Okay. We got this."

I pushed through the black drape, stumbled out from backstage and rushed out into the hallway. I was instantly dripping with sweat. Breathe, Scott, breathe.

I clicked Rebecca's name and held the phone to my ear. It rang twice and stopped. Silence.

"Hello?" The pounding of my heartbeat took over my whole body. More silence; then a quiet sigh drifted over the phone speaker.

"Hi." Dead air.

I swallowed hard. My mouth was completely dry. I took a deep breath—with the little bit of oxygen I had left in me—and verbalized my previous question... "Are you having an affair?"

"Yes."

The power of that one word hit me so hard in the chest that it literally knocked me off my feet. I fell backward through the air and landed with a thud, barely missing the hotel furniture next to me. It was like Apollo Creed had just rung my bell with a massive sucker punch. I couldn't feel anything. I stared at the ceiling for a moment. Instinctively, I grabbed the cushion of the chair to my right and pulled myself up. My face was laying in the seat when I asked what felt like the next obvious question...

"Who is it?"

"I'm not going to tell you."

"No. Really. Who is it?"

"Scott. I'm not going to tell you."

My emotions were everywhere and nowhere at the same time. This was a make-or-break moment. If I replied angrily and lashed out it would more or less be over. I made it to one knee. I was devastated yet oddly calm at the same time—can you say Holy Spirit? It was more about Him than me.

"Well. That's kinda crazy to hear. Do you want a divorce?"

"I don't know."

"Listen. I'm not mad at you and I'm not mad at him. We just need to figure this out."

"Okay. I don't know what to do. I feel relieved that I told you. I can breathe again."

"I get it. I understand. I'd like to come home and talk. If you want me to come home."

"Yes. That would be okay."

"I'm going to see about flying back in the morning. Please give me time to get there."

"Okay."

The call ended. I dropped into the chair in front of me. The only way to describe it is to say that I was just blank. I guess I was going into shock. No thoughts. No feelings. Just barely there.

After a while I staggered back into the ballroom and met up with my co-workers.

"Scott! You look awful. What happened?!?" Paula reached out to me.

"You should see the other guy." I exhaled and dropped my head onto Paula's shoulder. "Rebecca's having an affair. I need to go home and see what's going on."

"Oh no! I'm so sorry!" Paula hugged me. And there I stood backstage sobbing. I'm sure the crew had seen an emotional graphics operator before, but I can imagine, at that moment, they were thinking, "Could the client we're working for be THAT bad??"

On the drive home from the airport the worst-case scenario was going through my mind. "What if she's left and taken the kids with her? What do I do? What do I say? Where do I go?"

I drove through the neighborhood and came to a hard stop at the curb. I bolted out of the car and stopped at the entry way of our home. I was relieved to see that it didn't look deserted. As I braced myself to go in, I noticed the ancient intercom system on the brick wall to my right. It was like some sort of retro-tech communication device that would've fit right in on the set of the original 1960's Star Trek series. It was a tan rectangle about a foot and a half long and six inches tall. It had a plastic front grill with a grouping of dials on the top left corner. It had made it through the Cold War, the great flood of ought 10 and a total rebuild of the property, but it was pretty much useless. You could push the buttons and try to talk to the other rooms in the house, but you couldn't really understand what was being said. You could only make out the hint of words. None of it made sense.

Over the last few months, Rebecca and I might as well have been speaking to each other from either side of that intercom. We were talking but everything was getting lost in translation. Our ears weren't accurately hearing what our voices were saying. I have no doubt that there was spiritual warfare involved—that's something I'll delve into in greater detail later in the book. Suffice it to say, once I mustered up enough courage to go in and face her it didn't go very well.

We sparred back and forth about anything and everything and didn't really get anywhere. She was deeply hurt by all the ridiculous sexual activities we had both participated in—the control she felt I had over her—and she certainly wasn't buying my conversion story. I was deeply hurt by the inflammatory revelation from the night before and I was realizing that there was no way I could convince her I had really changed—that would take time—but it didn't seem like we had much of that left.

She didn't trust me. She didn't feel any security with me. Our intimacy had broken down completely. No matter how many times I tried to remind her that "we were a good team and had a ministry together" it rang hollow. I obviously hadn't been too concerned about "ministry" over the past two years. In her mind, all of this was just a desperate attempt on my part to save our marriage —and ultimately save face with our friends and family.

Over the course of the next few days we would have more painful interactions. There's one day that I remember vividly. We decided to take a walk together around the neighborhood. It was dusk and the light breeze made it feel like hammock weather. We were cordial enough toward each other—almost relaxed even. Not bad, considering. As the walk ended and we re-entered our cul-de-sac she confided in me that she was trying to decide if she was going to stay with me or not. In response, I moved in very close to her and held out my hands.

"Can we pray together?"

"No."

I was trying to hot-wire our spiritual connection, but she wasn't having it.

Her well had run dry towards me and there wasn't much I could do to refill it on my own.

That flat-out hard "No" in the middle of the street as the sun set majestically behind the trees was one of the hardest moments for me in a long list of hard moments.

After my wakeup call just a couple of weeks earlier, I was convinced that—whether our relationship survived or not—the most important thing either of us could do was rekindle our individual fellowship with God. It was gut-wrenching when it became obvious that, for now, Rebecca just didn't seem ready to do that.

Have you ever heard the one about the Longhorn, the Rabbi and the Reverend Smokin' Joe Frazier? Okay. Not a real joke. It does have potential, though. I'll let you work on that. Let me know what you come up with.

That phrase describes three men—three men who helped me through hard times. God so richly blessed me with these individuals. Each one of them offered a different aspect of accountability—or as I prefer to think of it, authenticity.

When life gets tough, we tend to gravitate toward the cheerleaders around us. "You can do it!" "You got this!" "You're awesome!" When life is hard, we don't necessarily want to hear about the fact that some of the mess might very well be of our own making. We just want to know it's all going to be all right and we'd like to avoid any discomfort along the way to victory.

God is love. That's so true. But He's also holy, just, perfect, faithful, truth, grace... I could go on and on! He's that awesome! He has so many spectacular qualities! When we get transfixed on just one of His attributes— because it's maybe the one that's most palatable to our senses or requires the least amount of change on our parts—then we short-circuit the healing and fullness of life He has prepared for us.

The authenticity that I encountered and enjoyed with these men manifested itself in complementary ways. The truth, grace and love they modeled helped spur me on toward a deeper understanding of God—even when it hurt.

THE LONGHORN. Dan is one of the biggest Texas Longhorn fans you could ever meet. So much so that I've often wondered why he ever left Austin! Burnt orange is a primary color to him. And even though that color can be a challenge for some he's always "lookin' good" when he wears it!

During the traumatic stretch from late 2010 to early 2011, Dan would swing by regularly and pick me up. We'd get a cup of coffee or—on those days when my nerves were more on edge—we would just drive around listening to music together. He was very patient and listened so well. At the same time, he didn't shy away from sharing TRUTH with me. He didn't get lost in the emotions I was sharing. He kept our conversations focused on my responsibility in—and God's sovereignty over—everything that was going on. A couple of verses that he consistently hit me with were truly significant...

"No discipline seems pleasant at the time, but painful. Later on, however, it produces a harvest of righteousness and peace for those who have been trained by it. Therefore, strengthen your feeble arms and weak knees. 'Make level paths for your feet,' so that the lame may not be disabled, but rather healed."
HEBREWS 12:11-13

My actions had consequences. The collapse of my marriage was directly linked to my poor behavior. The fact that I was experiencing the effects of my bad decisions didn't mean that God didn't love me. To the contrary, it meant that He did love me! For anything to grow the soil has to be broken and the seeds planted. Discipline breaks down immaturity, fosters growth and, ultimately, gives life to freedom. I'll always be thankful for the tough words that Dan shared with me. The truth he spoke into me pierced through my pride, settled deep inside my core and, to this day, influences the choices I make.

THE RABBI. Rick is a Messianic Jew who grew up in Brooklyn. He became a Jesus follower when he was 22 and since 1961 he has been an extraordinary Bible teacher. He and his wife Pat have modeled Christ's love to so many people—day in and day out.

There was a time in the Spring of 2011 when I called Rick before I boarded a plane home to see if he would meet me near the airport after I landed. He didn't hesitate. He just asked, "Where do you need me to be?" A few hours later we met in a hotel lobby just outside of DFW airport. I told him everything. I laid out the grisly details. He absorbed all of it, prayed over me and invited me to come over to his house. We sat in his living room and he showered me with valuable words of wisdom. Since I hadn't slept in a few days he let me lie down in his office and sleep for a few hours.

I'd shared my awful mistakes and in return I was simply offered a loving place to rest. Rick utilized his wonderful gifts to extend God's GRACE to a worn-out mess of a man. I don't know what I would've done without him. That small respite from the storm gave me the strength to make it through the days and weeks to come.

"Each of you should use whatever gift you have received to serve others, as faithful stewards of God's grace in its various forms."
1 PETER 4:10

THE REVEREND SMOKIN' JOE FRAZIER. Greg was the pastor of the local church we were attending at the time. He's a former music teacher and quite the violinist. He counseled me through the early months of 2011. On one occasion, he even made a house call when two of my tires blew out en route to his office. We met on the median outside the church as the tow truck loaded up my vehicle. In our sessions, Greg took a lot of time to walk me through the steps necessary to avoid the pitfalls of depression during these tumultuous times.

I would find out that this passive, artistic intellectual also had a bit of a violent streak! I vividly recall telling him about a moment of temptation backstage at a work event. It was a few months after I had decided to stop drinking. A glass of wine had been left sitting next to my computer. I glanced at it and a voice inside my head said, "You're backstage behind the curtain. No one would know." I quickly shut down my computers, put them away and skedaddled away from that glass as quickly as I could!

Greg understood alcohol was a gateway drug for me. His desk chair creaked as he leaned forward— an angry glint in his eye. "Scott. If I ever hear that you're drinking again I will come to your doorstep, knock on your door and punch you right in the face!" HashtagSubtle.

With comments like that Greg was actually showing copious amounts of LOVE to me! He cared so much that he was willing to go to great lengths to disciple me—whether it offended me or not! He was literally living out the words of 2 TIMOTHY 4:2...

"Preach the word; be prepared in season and out of season; correct, rebuke and encourage—with great patience and careful instruction."

Ever since then I've referred to him as the "Reverend Smokin' Joe Frazier"—in reference to the former heavyweight champion boxer who engaged in an intense rivalry with Muhammad Ali in the 1970s— and we've both laughed about it a lot over the years!

The "tough love" he displayed was a clear reminder that I needed to stay open to the freedom God had given me. I had a choice not to do certain things— like drinking alcohol—not as an act of works to impress God but as an act of obedience to worship Him. And, if I couldn't remember that on my own, Greg would be there to give me a swift sock in the face just in case!

God brought these men strategically into my life to help mold me and prep me at the right time. He knew that I was going to need Him—ALL of Him—for what lay ahead. No matter how hard loneliness would try its best to envelop me I understood that I would never be alone!

April 6, 2011... I knew it was going to happen, I just didn't know exactly when. We'd been trying to do counseling for a month or so but it wasn't going very well. Rebecca was thinking about leaving and I was thinking about staying. Our contradictory personal agendas were obviously not meshing well. As we headed home from a session in late March Rebecca had matter-of-factly announced that she had never really loved me and wanted a divorce. That was an out-of-body experience for sure. Life had been very disorienting since then.

And so, on my 41st birthday, it finally happened. It was about mid-morning and we were alone in the house. She came around the corner and met me in the center of the living room. Without making eye contact, she stood silently in front of me and handed me a manila envelope. I untwisted the brads and pulled out a packet of papers. At the top of the first page it said, "Original Petition for Divorce." My heart jumped up into my throat and I suddenly had an overwhelming urge to throw up.

At that point, Rebecca tried to get past me to go outside to the back yard. I stepped over and got in her way. "On my birthday?!? Really?!?" She asked that I let her by and—after an awkward stare down—I stepped aside. She made her way to the back porch as I thumbed through the paperwork.

Wow. It felt like someone was carving out my insides with a dull teaspoon. After a brief perusal, I slipped the document back into the envelope and placed it on my lap. I peered down at my gift and thought, "Happy birthday to me!"

A few days earlier I'd asked Rebecca if she'd join me and the boys to celebrate my birthday, so in an ironic twist, once everyone got home from school, we all went out for dinner and bowling. We were really pushing the boundaries of awkward to new levels!

Rebecca and I kinda played it off well, I guess. The boys seemed clueless. We made it through the evening and put the boys to bed; then we both lay down as far apart as we could on our bed and pretended to sleep.

I realized that it would probably be a good idea for me to contact a lawyer. I asked around and ended up at a family law office in Fort Worth. My sister— who suddenly showed up in town from North Carolina to offer moral support—went to the appointment with me. We walked in on a group of six men finishing up a Bible study. They ended in prayer and dispersed. The lawyer we were meeting with greeted us and led us into one of the side rooms lining the main office area.

My sister and I squirmed in our seats on one side of the conference table while the lawyer reviewed the divorce papers on the other. He flipped over the last page and looked up at me.

"You can fight all of this, you know."

"Uhm. What do you mean?"

"This document is pretty much not giving you much of a leg to stand on."

"Nice." I grimaced.

"You could take this to court and through your testimony you could balance this out quite a bit."

"Hmm. I don't think I want to do that. I don't want to rehash this whole story in public. I don't want to put her or the kids through that."

"Okay. Can I tell you what I think?"

"Uhm. Sure." I'm thinking *That's why we're here.*

"She's a hairdresser, right?"

"Yes, sir."

He went on to describe Rebecca's personality to a tee and then added, "I can tell you right now that she's getting all kinds of different opinions about this from her clients and friends."

"Okay."

"And she told you that the affair she was having was over?"

"Yes, sir." She had been quite adamant about that several times.

"Well, it's not. She's got a lot of voices going on inside her head. It's probably really very confusing for her right now."

"Okay." I looked over at my sister. The look on her face told me that she too just wanted to climb under the table and hide. I turned back to the lawyer. "So, what do you think I should do?"

"You should reconcile."

"What?!" That's the last thing I ever expected him to say!

"You should reconcile."

"Reconcile to WHAT?!?!"

Cue awkward silence. Then after a beat the lawyer continued. "I'd like you to seriously consider reconciling; but if you'd still like my services, I'll need a deposit."

My head was spinning. This man I had never met had pretty much just given us a complete character study of Rebecca—and his only clue to go on was the line in the divorce decree saying that she was a hair stylist. I'll admit, kind of impressive. But instead of urging me to pay him to start the divorce proceedings he was urging me to reconcile. What on earth was going on here??

After a quick double take, I asked him for the amount of the deposit, he told us, and my sister wrote a check to help me pay for it. He informed us that he was going to work up an updated document that would give me better legal footing. Once he was done with that, I would present it to Rebecca and her lawyer. As we left, he gave me the most comforting look and said, "I'll start this up for you; but if you decide not to pursue this, I'll tear up the check and you'll owe me nothing. I just want to let you know that."

My inner monologue said, "Dude, you're crazy town!" But my mouth said, "All right. Sounds good. Thank you!" I walked out of there pretty flustered. The words he shared kept echoing through my mind.

The next day Rebecca requested that we separate. She said she and the kids would move out of the house if necessary. I told her that was silly, and I assured her that I would find an apartment.

Once the new paperwork came in, Rebecca and her lawyer reviewed it and approved it. We had settled on joint custody. We would be splitting time with the kids evenly so we had to wrangle over the times and dates of how that would work. I don't think either one of us particularly enjoyed that part of the process. It felt so unfair to our unsuspecting young boys. At one point, I even asked her, "Why are we doing all of this?" She didn't respond.

I was still holding onto a faint hope of reconciliation, but the way things were looking, I had to continue to prepare myself for the worst. The next step we were about to take would prove to be the most disturbing. We decided that once I got back from my upcoming work trip to Miami, we would have one final family meeting to let our boys know that our marriage was ending.

DEMOLITION DAY

I think we can all agree that there's not a shortage of home improvement shows on TV. You can flip it or flop it or fix it up or hunt it or love it or list it! The various combinations seem endless. One of the most enjoyable parts of these shows—for the hosts especially—is "Demolition Day"!

It's the day where all of the planning comes to fruition and it's time to BUST STUFF UP! The sledgehammers and crow bars come out! That old look has gotta go! The hosts karate kick through walls—even jump through them if the opportunity arises! It's a free-for-all of destruction that allows all of that pent-up action movie angst to come flowing out! It honestly looks like a blast to participate in and it's fun to watch!

Demolition Day for our family, on the other hand, wasn't quite so fun. It would prove to be a day unlike any other. It was utterly brutal.

April 15, 2011... I slogged thru the Miami Airport. It felt like I was dragging around cinder blocks. Each step was harder than the next. I'd been texting and calling friends since I had crawled out of bed. I wanted the next two days to be bathed in prayer. I was asking that everyone involved be lifted up—specifically the boys.

D-Day was fast approaching for the Hardie family.

Soon our world would be flipped upside down and we would all be left dangling precariously on the edge of the unknown. Nothing would ever be the same.

I stared at the seat back in front of me during the entire flight. After the plane landed, I dragged myself off the plane, made it to baggage claim to retrieve my bags and then hauled all of my stuff to the car. Everything was moving in slow motion. None of it felt real.

On the way to check the status of my new apartment—secured just a few days earlier—I stopped by Walmart to pick up some spiral notebooks and pencils for the boys. Once we hit them with the news, I wanted them to be able to write down their thoughts and draw pictures about their feelings. It seemed like a healthy way to start processing such a massive life change.

By late afternoon, I made it to the house. I "slept" on the couch. At dawn my feet hit the floor and I was back on the phone. I had a good conversation with a friend who had gone through a similar situation recently. He walked me through potential scenarios, encouraged me and prayed for me. I checked in with another group of friends who were locked, loaded and ready to pray.

At 10am, Rebecca gathered the kids into the living room. I texted my friends, "PRAY NOW!" and made my way from the bedroom. I sat in the love seat directly opposite the couch where Rebecca and the boys were huddled. Drew, Jake and Alex were 12, 10 and 8.

"First off, guys, I love each of you and Mom very much. No matter what happens that will never change. I've done things that have really hurt Mom and it's just too much for us to make it through. I feel really terrible about all of it. I ask for your forgiveness. I'm so sorry! Mom has something to say now..."

I had let Rebecca know that I wasn't on board with the divorce so I couldn't be the one to tell them. We both agreed she would do it. She tried to make eye contact with each of them as she spoke.

"I love you very much. Like Dad said, we've both done some really hard things and I need to tell you something..." Her voice quivered and she stopped for a moment. "Your dad and I will be separating. He's got a new apartment and will be moving there. We will all go over there today to see that. I love you all SO much!"

Drew and Jake burst into tears. Alex stared straight ahead. Rebecca pulled Jake and Alex close to her and I moved over to comfort Drew. A few moments later I pulled out the notebooks and handed one to each of them.

"I know this is really, really tough. We got these notebooks for you to write in and draw pictures in. It can be about anything you're feeling today."

Rebecca sat with Jake and Alex as they started working in their notebooks. Drew and I wandered out to the back porch where we talked for quite a while. He was trying to process everything. I shared the story without going into any gory details and answered all of his questions as best as I could.

Later that afternoon we all went over to my new apartment. It was a two bedroom/two bath. The back bedroom would be mine; Jake and Alex would have two beds in the middle bedroom and Drew would man the pullout couch in the living room. My mom and sister had helped me furnish the apartment on short notice. It was modest but comfortable.

After a very brief tour we made our way down to the clubhouse and swimming pool. We went back and forth between swimming, messing about in the small fitness center and playing billiards.

The boys seemed to be enjoying themselves. They're resilient dudes. It's weird. The whole time I just felt the sensation of love. In response I wanted to convey love to Drew, Jake, Alex and Rebecca. Christ was most definitely present and active.

At sunset we headed back to the house. While the boys were getting ready for bed, Rebecca and I had a private moment in the master bathroom. I asked her if I could pray for her and she said, "Yes." I prayed, she thanked me and then I headed to Drew's room.

I passed Jake and Alex in the kitchen as they were en route to the master bedroom to bunk with Rebecca for the night. I gave them each a hug and told them I loved them.

I slipped quietly into Drew's room. He was sitting up in his bed with his Bible on his lap.

"Hey, D."

"Dad."

"What's up?"

"I need you to read this." Drew held out his Bible and placed his finger where I should start. PROVERBS 23:27-33 [I'm using The Message version here]...

"Dear child, I want your full attention; please do what I show you. A whore is a bottomless pit; a loose woman can get you in deep trouble fast. She'll take you for all you've got; she's worse than a pack of thieves."

Ouch.

"Whose eyes are bleary and bloodshot? It's those who spend the night with a bottle, for whom drinking is serious business. Don't judge wine by its

94

label, or its bouquet, or its full-bodied flavor. Judge it rather by the hangover it leaves you with—the splitting headache, the queasy stomach. Do you really prefer seeing double, with your speech all slurred, reeling and seasick, drunk as a sailor?"

Ouch squared. I resembled these remarks. I handed the Bible back to him.

"You have to promise me you'll never do this stuff again."

"Dude. I promise."

"What about Mom? What happened with her?"

I texted Rebecca and told her she might want to come into Drew's room. A few moments later she was at Drew's bed side. He wanted her to look at the same verses. She did and handed the Bible back to Drew.

"I need y'all to promise you won't do this to each other again. Promise?" His glance went back and forth between us.

I nodded in agreement and Rebecca whispered, "Yes, Drew. I do."

Rebecca gave her son a hug and we all said, "Good night." Drew and I lowered ourselves down into sleeping position simultaneously. My head rested at one end of the bed and Drew's at the other.

"I love you, Drew."

"I love you, too, Dad."

I lay there exhausted but alert. Sensory overload made it impossible for me to turn my mind off. What a crazy day. My world was crumbling around me, but I'd never felt so in tune with the Lord. It didn't make any sense! If God was really with me why was everything so terrible? Was it worth it to keep following Him? Where do I go from here?

A guy named Asaph—and I thought my first name "Jeffrey" was bad—came to mind. He was one of King David's chief musicians who assisted in temple worship services. At one point in his life, he was going through dire straits of his own. He shared his feelings in PSALM 73. I've always been partial to Asaph. His musings are so raw—he's just being real—and that resonates with me. Even though it was a couple thousand years ago his sentiments prove to be timeless.

He was immersed in a world that he didn't understand. Certain people in his community were living in opposition to God. Yet, by all outward appearances, they seemed to be flourishing. It didn't compute in his mind and that troubled his heart. He questioned his faith. He questioned whether he should even bother continuing to pursue God at all [PSALM 73:13]. The physical evidence was telling him that his efforts at holiness were futile. Why go on? Why endure for the cause when the cause seemed to be so pointless?

After much soul-searching his mind was made up in verse 26...

"My flesh and my heart may fail, but God is the strength of my heart and my portion forever."

Asaph decided that he didn't want something FROM God, he just wanted GOD! It didn't matter if he was going to be celebrated or mocked. It didn't matter what everyone around him was doing or how life seemed to be treating him. What mattered was that God was with him and he was with God. That relationship wasn't just enough for him, it was everything to him!

When the reason you get up in the morning becomes irrelevant—when your family is shattered by divorce; when the job promotion you've wanted goes to someone else; when the kids you've invested in leave the nest; when the friend you've trusted betrays you— where do you go to find solace and purpose?

Could it be that you can find your purpose in God? That He can be enough when nothing else will do?

It was becoming clearer with each passing day that... "for me, it is good to be near God. I have made the Sovereign Lord my refuge; I will tell of all your deeds." [PSALM 73:28]

A decade earlier the previously mentioned verse 26 had become my personal life verse. It accurately summed up my faith experience and became my mantra, my prayer. On that night, bunking with my oldest son in his deceptively comfortable double bed, it would be the lifeline I would cling to to make it through the night. It would calm my fears, soothe my mind and allow me to rest. My heart and my flesh were most definitely failing but God was holding me together.

My eyes began to close, and sleep crept over me quickly. Just like that one of the most challenging days of my life became a haunting memory. It was

Saturday evening. On Monday morning I was set to move out for good.

POWER RESTORED

Have you ever experienced a power outage at your home? It's nerve-racking, right? In a bad weather scenario, you at least have a chance to prep for the occasion. You can check your favorite weather app and see the trajectory and speed of the storm. Based on that info you can guesstimate the storm's ETA. In the meantime, you can gather all your available light resources—flashlights and candles—and put them in one central location. Add an emergency charge of your phone and you're well-prepared to make it through the night.

It's always startling when the lights finally start flickering. A flash of panic... a quick double check of supplies... and then... fwooooosh... the power goes out! Pretty stressful situation!

You can double the anxiety when the blackout hits unexpectedly. You're minding your own business and BOOM lights out! I don't know about you, but my first reaction is to venture outside to see how much of the surrounding area has been affected—partly out of concern for the neighbors and partly out of an irrational fear that I may have forgotten to pay the electric bill.

What if the blackout didn't just take out your neighborhood but it took out your city or your entire state? How much would that move the needle on your personal Freak-Out Meter? It's hard to imagine but it has happened before.

On August 14, 2003, the northeastern United States—and sections of southeastern Canada—experienced the largest blackout in U.S. history.

A power surge somewhere near Ontario affected the transmission grid at 4:10pm EDT. For the next 30 minutes outages were reported in parts of Ohio, New York, Michigan and New Jersey. Soon major cities like Cleveland, Akron, Toledo, Baltimore, Rochester, Syracuse, Albany, New York City, Detroit, Hartford and Toronto were left without power.

Eventually a triangular area of seven U.S. states and a large swath of southern Ontario were affected! That's a grand total of 55 MILLION people embroiled in an event of epic proportions!

It was a hot day—88 degrees in New York City alone—and the heat played a role in the initial surge that had triggered the wider power outage. The high temperatures increased energy demand as people across the region turned on their fans and A/C units. This caused the power lines to sag as higher currents heated the lines, putting more pressure on the electrical infrastructure, which ultimately caved in.

After the catastrophic system failure, the weather caused immediate health concerns among senior citizens and smaller children, who were having difficulties dealing with the elements. The trouble didn't stop there.

Shocked workers rushed out of skyscrapers and office buildings, flooding the streets. With stoplights out, traffic became a massively confusing gridlock. Essential services remained operational for some areas but for others backup generation systems failed. Water systems in several cities lost pressure, forcing boil water advisories to be put into effect. Cell service was interrupted as mobile networks were overloaded with calls. Railways were shut down and planes were grounded. The power outage's effects on international air transport and financial markets were widespread. Fortunately—with the help of backup generators—most television and radio stations were able to remain on the air to disseminate information to a panicked populace.

For some, power was restored by 11pm that same night; but for most it took up to 48 hours [Information gathered from cbs.com].

The ramifications of the power outage were expansive and, in some cases, devastating. During my research, one very interesting aftereffect stood out to me. In the big cities where power remained off after nightfall, the Milky Way became visible. It must've been an inspiring spectacle for people who—because of particulate air and light pollution—didn't ordinarily get to see the stars! When all of the distractions were stripped away, they were able to experience the handiwork of the Creator of the universe! God's beauty illuminated the darkness. Despite the pain and inconvenience, it was an amazing once-in-a-lifetime opportunity for so many!

The accumulated stress of one terrible decision after another had short-circuited our family. The elements had pressed down on us and our systems had faltered under the stress. The power was out. On a lifeless Saturday evening an all-consuming blackout enveloped us as we slept.

Around 3am—during the darkest of night—the bedroom door cracked open and a glimmer of light cut across my face.

"Scott?" Rebecca whispered.

"Yeah?"

"I have a terrible migraine. Would you mind rubbing my head?"

Given the events of the previous day this was a strange request, but I was up for it. I replied softly, "Sure, babe."

Without a second thought, I hopped out of bed and followed her into the living room. I sat in the recliner and Rebecca sat on the floor in front of me. We sat in silence as I rubbed her head. After two hours, Rebecca cleared her throat. In the moment before she uttered her next words, I can imagine the angels in heaven took a deep breath in anticipation. She turned her head slightly toward me—her chin resting on her shoulder—and said...

"If you are who you say you are...
I want you to stay."

My lips tightened into an almost imperceptible grin. The intent of the message was clear. God was reminding me that the mistakes I'd made were what I was capable of but not who I was. I was who HE said I was. A child of God. A sinner redeemed. Fear could no longer imprison me—I was free. My hands stopped, my head lowered, my eyes closed, and I quietly replied, "I want to stay."

With four simple words heaven couldn't take it anymore! The angels burst into celebration! God's glory exploded into reality and the shadows were lit up!

"The light shines in the darkness, and the darkness can never extinguish it."
JOHN 1:5 [NLT]

You might think I'm speaking in hyperbole when I describe the heavenly reaction to this crazy little scene being played out in a recliner in the dead of night. Based on what Jesus tells us in LUKE 15:10 [TPT] I'm pretty sure I nailed it...

"That's the way God responds every time one lost sinner repents and turns to him. He says to all his angels, 'Let's have a joyous celebration, for that one who was lost I have found!'"

Heaven isn't a stiff stained-glass mural hidden away in some far-off remote location. It's a vibrant active place where the divine remains intimately involved in the events taking place in the here and now.

Jesus had been with us through everything. We had been unable to see Him because our vision was blurred by all the debris in the atmosphere around us. Once the lights were completely shut off—when our darkest moment had come upon us—we were able to experience His beauty in the most extravagant of ways.

I was totally unaware of the internal battle that Rebecca had been going through all night. Jesus had stirred her, and they had been wrestling for hours. She knew that God had seen enough, and she was exhausted by all of the drama as well. There could be no rest until things were put back on the right course. Sandwiched in the bed between Jake and Alex she got on her phone and ended the affair with the other person. Now the main sticking point left to resolve was how she would go about telling me that she wanted me to stay.

She desired to tell me in her own words, but God kept insisting she use others. She didn't understand. They went back and forth until Rebecca finally released control and used the words God wanted me to hear.

After our brief exchange we didn't really say anything else to each other. I gave her shoulders one last squeeze, leaned my head against hers and gave her a soft kiss on the top of her head. Rebecca got up from the floor and walked back to the master bedroom. I pushed myself out of the recliner and adjourned to Drew's room.

The boys and I were at the dining room table in the kitchen eating breakfast—and I was kinda wondering where Rebecca was—when her voice drifted out from the master bedroom, "Morning, guys!" When I heard it, I immediately knew things had truly changed. Her voice simply sounded different than it had sounded over the last several months. She was back! And that helped me realize that last night hadn't been a dream after all! As she came into the room and I stood up to greet her. She looked at me, took my hand and we both turned toward the boys.

"Guys. We want y'all to know that things have changed. Dad isn't going anywhere! He's staying!"

The boys lifted their cereal spoons high into the air and erupted into a simultaneous cheer: "YEEESSS!"

Rebecca and I stepped away from the table. She faced me and we stared at each other with equal portions of disbelief and relief. We slowly erased the gap between us, extended our arms and embraced for what seemed like the first time in forever.

Now that the lights were back on it was time to see what our new normal would look like. We were about to experience a lot of hard things on the road to healing. We were about to see what happens after the miracle—after the happily ever after.

...PART TWO...

FIXER UPPER

Miracles are wonderful! When God does something unexplainable it's easy to get our praise on! We clap harder, our arms raise higher and our voices get louder! But once the dust settles and the euphoric high is replaced by the daily routine, where do we go from there?

I wish it was as easy as sharing a 1-2-3-This-Is-How-We-Do-It-Checklist on how to rebuild a relationship overnight. But it's a massive project with an overwhelming number of variables that takes time, patience and grit. If it could only be as easy as rebuilding a house—or at least how we see the rebuilding being done on those trendy home improvement shows! How can they make something as intricate and labor intensive as remodeling a home look SO easy? Here's a quick breakdown of how it's done...

The Home Improvement TV Show Checklist:

✓ Find a really messed up property that nobody wants.

- ✓ Entice an eager couple to buy it.
- ✓ Design a brand spanking new home on the laptop with a few clicks of the mouse.
- ✓ Edit 90 days of back-breaking work into a 10-minute video montage.
- ✓ VOILÀ! Reveal the new home!

In 40 minutes, the money pit has become a palace and the new homeowners didn't even have to lift a finger in the process! But what about the months of hard work cut out of the final edit? The bumps, bruises, blood, sweat and tears involved in construction work—hauling and hanging sheet rock, hammering nail after nail, lifting hefty packs of shingles to the roof, sprawling on the ground cutting and placing carpet, clearing brush, shifting mounds of dirt from one place to the other, the doing and the redoing!

There's not much glamour in the real day-to-day remodeling of a home nor is there in the moment-by-moment rebuilding of a relationship. You can't make any quick edits or take any shortcuts. If you do, then it can all come tumbling down and bury everything under an avalanche of regret.

As Rebecca and I started the arduous task of rebuilding we didn't have a magic blueprint at our fingertips. It would've been so nice to go instantly from groundbreaking to grand re-opening. But as we leveled the dirt and restored the foundation of our marriage, we needed to take some very important steps. It all felt a bit improvisational at the time; but in retrospect, I have no doubt that God was moving us through a very definitive process. Here's a quick thumbnail of what we experienced...

The Relationship Rebuild Checklist:

- ✓ **Face2Face:** Clean the slate, focus on the best and let go of the rest.
- ✓ **Back2Back:** Circle up, back-to-back, swords drawn and identify the real enemy.
- ✓ **Mind2Heart:** Take time to heal and learn to discern feelings vs. reality.

- ✓ **Why2What:** Know the Why to do the What, and obedience has its rewards.
- ✓ **Old2New:** Don't put another brick in the wall and be all in.

I'd like to take you on a tour of the rebuild. We'll walk through each step of the process. I hope you'll find the journey useful and encouraging. Just a friendly reminder before we get started: construction sites can be messy and dangerous so please keep your arms and legs inside the vehicle at all times! Ready? Set? Let's go!

FACE2FACE

We'd come a long way overnight—from officially announcing our divorce one morning to embracing like long-lost lovers the next. If you haven't noticed by now the Hardies don't do things in the most orthodox manner. We're not quite sure what normal is. Perhaps God has built that flexibility into our personalities for a reason. Our comfort level with awkward situations probably helped us immensely as we bobbed and weaved our way through the mine field ahead of us.

One of the first land mines we encountered was the fallout from Rebecca's affair. My sexual dalliances had been out there on display for a while. It was all common knowledge by this point. The affair was a different animal. It had been a volatile undercover operation and its discovery had the potential to derail not one but two families.

I'm not going to go into too much detail here. But, suffice it to say, I knew more about what was going on than Rebecca realized. In the weeks leading up to D-Day I'd uncovered enough evidence to know who the other person was. I couldn't quite figure out what I was going to do with that information. My first thought was confrontation. I would gather everyone together and unveil the culprit with a witty biting monologue! Like the climactic scene in a murder mystery I would exclaim, "AH-HA!" and melodramatically point to the suspect from across the room! Yeah. I know. Probably not the most mature way to handle it.

Betrayal conjures up a deep lasting pain that isn't easy to overcome. I can only tell you how I decided to come to grips with it. I prayed. And after that I prayed some more. And then some more after that. I knew the Holy Spirit needed to be in control because if it was left in my hands, I was going to make a real mess of it. I took it to the Lord. He listened and the path I should take became quite evident. Instead of provoking the situation, I needed to wait.

This might not be the appropriate reaction for everyone in a similar situation; but in this case, it was the right thing to do. In order for the process of reconciliation to gain traction we didn't need an " I gotcha" moment, we needed a brutally honest confessional moment. This would help kickstart my ability to trust again and, at the same time, confirm that Rebecca's willingness to work on our marriage was genuine.

Soon after our Sunday morning celebration with the boys my patience would be rewarded. Rebecca and I drove over to a local car wash. Car maintenance was a good excuse to have a private conversation. We sat on a bench on the patio outside the storefront of the car wash. Rebecca's voice trembled and tears streamed out from under her sunglasses as she told me about the affair. I caressed her shoulder as she spoke. I couldn't overreact or cut her off. I had to let her get it all out. When she finished, she simply asked, "Are you going to leave me now?" This was a pivotal moment. I sat up taller and removed my sunglasses.

"I knew what was going on. I've been waiting for you. I love you and I'm not going anywhere."

A deep breath engulfed her entire body as she leaned over onto me and began to sob. I held her until the car wash worker swung the white towel over his head letting us know it was time to go. Our hands overlapped on the center console as we drove a few blocks to Rebecca's salon. She came around to the driver side window and waited for the whirr of the automatic window to stop before she spoke.

"Thank you for staying."

My emotions left me at a loss for words, so I just offered an affirmative nod in reply. She gently patted the car door and headed into work.

"Above all, love each other deeply, because love covers over a multitude of sins."
1 PETER 4:8

Here's the deal. I couldn't make my decision after

Rebecca's confession. I had to know my response ahead of time so that the emotions of the moment would have no effect on my answer. I was already locked in for the long haul. And, trust me, it was going to be a loooong haul!

As I've mentioned before, if you're going to build anything you have to start by clearing away the brush. You've got to remove anything that might impede the construction process and affect the integrity of the structure once it's complete.

The first thing Rebecca and I had to do was CLEAN THE SLATE. We'd both hurt each other. The pain was intense, and it was definitely going to leave a mark. We couldn't just act like nothing had happened. Our history had taught us how devastating that could be. Peacekeeping wasn't going to allow us to be successful. We had to embrace our newfound identities as Peacemakers!

That meant we couldn't just shrug it off and bottle it up. We had to open it up and let it out. It had to be a complete soul cleansing. We couldn't hold onto one hurt and release the other; we had to willingly tie it all up with one big bow and give it away.

We needed help. It was imperative that we find a third party to help mediate our conversations. We turned to counseling once again. A friend recommended a Biblical counselor whose office wasn't too far from our home. His name is Dell and, man, did he ever turn out to be a Godsend! Without his perceptive advice, sincere prayers and constant reliance on Scripture I don't know if our marriage would've survived, much less thrived!

Unlike our first foray into the counseling world, this time around we were both on the same page—we were united in our desire to stay together.

In order to stay together we would have to wipe away the dirt and grime so that we would have a clean, healthy place for our love to grow. Cleaning the slate in such a way would set the stage for us to rebuild trust.

Because of my terrible behavior over the preceding couple of years Rebecca still had her doubts about me. That seems natural considering everything that had gone down. She had to realize—and believe—that I was different now. She would encounter the changes in the smallest of ways. For instance, when I would eagerly try a new food without any complaints—I was a notoriously picky eater in the past—it would baffle her and she would cock her head to one side and say, "Who ARE you?!" She had to experience that kind of mind-altering change on a consistent basis to continue to bolster her renewed confidence and trust in me.

I was working through my own trust issues as well. I was dealing with the insidious aftereffects of betrayal, and the only way I was going to be victorious was to forgive and forget.

It's essential to remember that while forgetting will happen LATER forgiving needs to happen NOW!

No matter how many times the memories came back to haunt me, I had to choose to let go of any right to get even or exact revenge. Dell advised me to pray for the other person that had been involved in the affair. That might sound crazy, but it was quite constructive! I could've easily locked myself into a prison of resentment, but I would have been the only one rotting behind those bars. Offering daily prayers for someone who had damaged my heart so profoundly was actually a gigantic step in the healing process for me! I'll have more to say about that in the **Mind2Heart** section.

As we worked to clean our slates we also had to FOCUS ON THE BEST AND LET GO OF THE REST! In the beginning stages of a relationship the object of our infatuation can do no wrong. We love everything about them! How in the world does this perfect human exist?! With time comes knowledge and with knowledge comes familiarity—which invariably opens our eyes to disappointment.

"Oh man! She loves Stevie Nicks but can't stand Phil Collins! Could this be a deal breaker?" Probably not. Over time, music preferences can be altered or, at the very least, tolerance can be cultivated. Rebecca has grown to appreciate Phil and I've learned to listen to Stevie without making any disparaging remarks. So, there is hope!

As the intimacy level deepens, it's important to be realistic about a potential mate. You've got to establish non-negotiables—those things that make pursuing a deeper commitment a no-go for you—and be willing to walk away if need be. At the same time, it's important to remember that the other person is as perfect as you are. Uhm. You know you're not perfect, right? Just checking.

We have to be aware that imperfection will always be a source of friction. I mean, think about it. The warning is right there in the middle of the vows shared at most weddings: "...to have and to hold, from this day forward, **for better, for worse...**"

Yeah. If you haven't experienced the worst yet, trust me, you will. It's just a matter of time.

Unfortunately, as a relationship matures it can be painfully easy to magnify the negatives and minimize the positives. I guess it's just a weird quirk of human nature, but it's not impossible to avoid this relationship trap.

I know that I spent far too much time—for far too many years—focusing on Rebecca's faults. And, more often than not, it would be a subtle jab that I thought nothing of that would actually hurt Rebecca the most. It was those "little things" that had built up and led us to the doorstep of failure.

Now that Rebecca and I had been given a fresh start, we appreciated each other so much more than ever before! We were by no means walking around with blinders on. There were important things to work on—and there always will be. But despite our failings, we were learning to adore each other more and more every day. That became a big deal for us.

When I was spending some time meditating on this concept of adoring each other, I decided to check out Dictionary.com. The definition I discovered for the word "adoration" was quite interesting...

Adoration: deep love and respect.

That takes us right back to EPHESIANS 5:33... "However, each one of you also must LOVE his wife as he loves himself, and the wife must RESPECT her husband." Coincidence? I think not.

I choose to FOCUS ON THE BEST in Rebecca because, honestly, there's so much there to appreciate! She is beautiful, witty, caring, generous, creative, industrious, and the list goes on and on. As I spend my energies adoring her, my love and respect grow exponentially. Her shortcomings and failures lose their significance and I'm free to LET GO OF THE REST!

We can't change the past. It's part of our story now. But we don't have to let the memories of who we were and what we did then drain the joy out of who we are and what we are doing now.

When all is said and done, we are two broken people who have cleaned the slate, focused on the best and let go of the rest. Despite being keenly aware of the good, the bad and the ugly we choose to be fearless; we choose to run toward each other; we choose to see each other through the eyes of a love that passes all understanding.

"And I pray that you, being rooted and established in love, may have power, together with all the Lord's holy people, to grasp how wide and long and high and deep is the love of Christ, and to know this love that surpasses knowledge—that you may be filled to the measure of all the fullness of God."
EPHESIANS 3:17-19

BACK2BACK

I'm sitting in my room at the Aria in Las Vegas. I find myself staring at the blank page in front of me. After a long day of work, I've been trying to get in the right mindset to talk about spiritual warfare. Since the topic lends itself so easily to the action movie genre, I've been cycling through action movie soundtracks in iTunes for inspiration.

After sampling quite a few albums I've zeroed in on *Captain America: The Winter Soldier Original Motion Picture Soundtrack* written by Henry Jackman and released by Hollywood Records in 2014. I'm drawn to the urgency and drive found in the songs. There's nothing passive about them. These songs are meant to take you somewhere. So much so that I suddenly have the irrational urge to leap from my 10th floor window, slide down to the rooftop below, parkour myself straight across the Vegas Strip and crash through a Planet Hollywood hotel window searching for bad guys!

If I were to actually survive that burst of super heroism, I'm pretty sure that I would find myself in trouble with the local authorities so, on second thought, I'd better not. Seriously though, I do love the vibe of this music. It oozes a contagious energy that simply makes you want to get up and do something! And that's exactly the mindset we should have when it comes to spiritual warfare!

The Scriptures tell us that there is a battle going on. The struggle between good and evil is real. We can see it played out in the headlines every day. We can sense the tension around us and within us. There's definitely a presence pushing against the things of God—an enemy with a personal vendetta is on the loose. The Scriptures give this enemy a name and that name is "Satan." In REVELATION 12 we're given a brief glimpse into his history.

He was once an angel under God's authority. But his pride got the best of him. His jealousy toward God inspired him to rebel. A war broke out in heaven and ultimately Satan lost. He and the angels that fought along aside him were thrown out of Heaven and cast down to earth.

Ever since then he and his minions have done everything in their power to mislead the world. He had his eye on Adam and Eve at the very beginning of time and he has his eye on you right now. He is arrogant, powerful, cruel and deceitful—the embodiment of total evil. He wants nothing more than to take you out. There's no reasoning with him; there's not going to be any negotiated cease-fire; he's on the offensive 24/7.

"Your enemy the devil prowls around like a roaring lion looking for someone to devour."
1 PETER 5:8

Rebecca and I were battered, bruised and exhausted. We knew that we had been through a battle of epic proportions and we felt it from head to toe. Satan had prowled around us, kicked down our door and barged right in. It had been a full-on home invasion!

In light of all that had happened we knew we couldn't stay where we were any longer. It just wasn't emotionally or spiritually beneficial. We soon realized that God had already put the wheels in motion to provide a place for us. That two-bedroom apartment that I was already paying for was just sitting there waiting for us. We packed up and moved into it as quickly as we could.

It was far from ideal, but we made it work. The boys just rolled with it. They were fans of the swimming pool and the clubhouse, so it was an upgrade in their minds!

The Avengers just popped into my head—not a huge surprise considering the music pumping out of my phone. I'm thinking about that classic scene in the first *Avengers* [Marvel Studios, 2012]. It's where the team comes together during the battle of New York. The enemy is overwhelming the city. If they don't do something fast, all will be lost. One by one our heroes circle up. The camera swirls dramatically around them as they regroup—back to back—preparing to go on the offensive. There's no doubting that the tables are about to turn. Captain America barks out a series of orders re-focusing the combined strength of the team. They have the power, the passion and the plan. The alien invaders are in their crosshairs and nothing is going to stop them from winning the battle. This is such a great picture of how we should handle spiritual warfare!

The enemy is very strategic. He studies us intently. He's like a commissioned officer reviewing top secret intel in a war room. He can see our reactions to people and situations. Does the hair on the back of her neck stand up? Does he take a secret second glance? He collects all of this personal data and uses it against us. You've got to remember that he's a master of sleight-of-hand tricks. He'll make you think he's going for your weakness when he's really laser-focused on your strength.

Rebecca and I thought we were strong—especially when it came to our sex life. There was no way we could have a problem in that arena. We were really good at it. We could start stretching the boundaries. What would be the harm in doing that? HashTagWeGotThis. See that big red flag of pride we were waving? It was basically a signal to the enemy to come get us! And, boy, did he ever! He essentially ignored our weaknesses and took aim at what we perceived as our greatest strength. He acquired the target, set his sights on the bullseye and let the bullets fly.

I don't think the enemy's #1 goal was to destroy our marriage or break apart our family or even ruin our lives per se—that was all just a treasure trove of fringe benefits. He was aiming at our core. He wanted to inflict maximum damage on our faith. He knew that if the chaos and confusion of sin took over our lives we would disconnect from God and he would have the opportunity to discredit the Creator. "See all of these things of God? They don't work!"

The story being played out in the physical realm was just a reflection of the battle that was being waged in the spiritual realm. Our intimacy was broken, our fellowship with God fractured. We were caught in the no man's land between the trenches of two opposing forces. That's where the deadliest battles of the war take place.

"For our struggle is not against flesh and blood, but against the rulers, against the authorities, against the powers of this dark world and against the spiritual forces of evil in the heavenly realms." EPHESIANS 6:12

To be victorious in this cosmic spiritual battle we have to CIRCLE UP BACK-TO-BACK! In the midst of the melee we need to establish and maintain a secure perimeter. Within that safe space we can protect each other's blind spots and develop our own plan of attack.

It's obvious that the enemy is quite methodical in his madness. If we don't respond with a methodical strategy of our own, then the battle will be lost.

For any soldier on the battlefront, communication is key. Each combatant needs to know the plan and their role in the plan. When an opposing army is able to cut off the other army's communications link with home base then it's much easier to surround, isolate and subdue their opponent. It's the same way on the spiritual battlefield. The enemy doesn't want us having any conversations with headquarters. The military has satellite phones and radios for communication. The Christian has prayer.

Rebecca and I realized that a vibrant prayer life was going to be essential for us. Without that lifeline to God we simply weren't going to make it.

The stakes were too high to be passive. We resolved to pray with each other every day. We couldn't just say we were going to pray or say that we had prayed—whether we had done it or not. Nope. That's not being strategic; that's just being lazy. We had to be intentional and set aside dedicated time each day to voice our prayers out loud together. We've made it a priority to diligently nurture and maintain this aspect of our lives. Even when we both took turns participating in a three-day Christian retreat that didn't allow phone usage, we wrote prayers for each other that we opened each day. The blessings and benefits of focusing on prayer are too numerous to count. But please don't get the wrong idea here—prayer isn't about accumulating blessings. Intimacy should be the primary goal of our ongoing conversations with God. Any blessing we receive should be seen as a byproduct of His provision for us and never as a substitute for relationship with Him.

The vitality of our covenant relationship with each other is directly tied to the quality of our fellowship relationship with Christ.

An active prayer life enables us to sustain and fortify a powerful defense against the advances of the enemy. But we can't perpetually stay in a defensive posture. As we circle up back-to-back, we have to have our SWORDS DRAWN, ready to go on the offensive and take the fight to the enemy!

Our adversary had attempted to take so much from us, and we had to let him know that, through the power of God's Word, we were going to be taking it all back—and then some!

EPHESIANS 6:17-18 tells us that we should take up "the sword of the Spirit, which is the Word of God. And pray in the Spirit on all occasions with all kinds of prayers and requests. With this in mind, be alert and always keep on praying..."

As we reestablished ourselves as a couple, we needed to apply the healing power of prayer to every part of our lives. Our sexual relationship was at the top of the list. The upsetting behaviors that had occurred over the last several months had obviously affected our ability to trust one another. Rebecca was hesitant to be intimate with me and I felt a little odd about it too. What would it be like? Would it ever be the same again?

The subject came up in one of our early sessions with Dell and his response was quite direct...

"You need to do it as soon as you get home!" Well, okay then! What do you really think?

He wasn't being flippant at all. We were both totally invested in our relationship. This was an amazing opportunity to rebuild our marriage into something that was even better than before. His concern was that if we waited too long to be sexually intimate the enemy could use that as a way to stir controversy and animosity between us.

He closed the session by saying, "I'm amazed at what I see here. There are no walls between you. It is so beautiful. You two are a trophy of God's grace." That wouldn't be the last time we would hear that particular phrase directed toward us.

It's weird. I'd come to terms with the fact that we might never be together again. Honestly, I didn't know if I would ever be with anyone again. I'd given my sexuality completely over to God. While I did miss being with my bride, I knew I was complete without it. I didn't need it to validate my personal worth or soothe any urgent physical need. Considering where I'd come from in regard to my sexuality, it was crazy to think that I was simply content.

The enemy had used my sordid infidelities and Rebecca's affair to cause a gigantic rift between us. The joy of becoming "one flesh" had been completely taken away from us. With our confidence firmly placed in God's Word we were going to retake the ground that had been lost.

It had been over four months since we had been sexually intimate with each other. We were both nervous. Could we physically engage each other without the pain of betrayal cluttering our minds? Could it once again be a beautiful picture of the goodness of God? Could it be a pure act of worship?

In response to a suggestion in our counseling session, I prayed for our lovemaking in advance. I vocalized my prayers as I lay next to Rebecca. "Lord, I ask that our minds would be clear. I ask that You would be honored and glorified. We thank You for the gift of intimacy. We thank You for being here with us. In Jesus' name, Amen."

I know. It seems a bit foreign—okay, probably downright strange—to include prayer as a part of the lovemaking process. I've gotten an assortment of peculiar looks as I've shared this over the years.

Why do we find this so unusual? Perhaps it's because we've spent so much time participating in the sexual act—something God specifically created for us to enjoy—without involving Him in the matter at all. In our conversations about sex, do we use words like, "bored" and "fantasize" instead of "worship" and "delight"? If so, we've lost touch with the true purpose of sex and, as a result, we aren't able to experience it to the fullest.

Let me tell ya... Prayer works! Rebecca and I had NO problems whatsoever! Our minds and bodies were free to enjoy the benefits of "one flesh" in a miraculous way! Ever since then I've continued to pray for our lovemaking. With all of our selfish motivations gone, our most intimate physical acts are given as a love offering to God and that binds the enemy from staking any claim in the process.

Husbands, I urge you to consider taking on the leadership role in this area. Allowing God to be present at the center of your sexual intimacy will change everything! I have no doubt that you'll think about sex differently, talk about sex differently and experience sex in a more fulfilling way.

"Bless your fresh-flowing fountain! Enjoy the wife you married as a young man! Lovely as an angel, beautiful as a rose—don't ever quit taking delight in her body. Never take her love for granted!" PROVERBS 5:18-19 [MSG]

Let's check back in with those Avengers for a sec.

When we last left them, they had just circled up together and were about to kick some alien butt during the Battle of New York. Ultimately, they enjoyed a decisive victory and saved the entire world from annihilation! Going through such a horrific crucible together must've developed some seriously deep and lasting bonds, right? How could you risk your lives for each other like that and not become BFFs??

Welp. Life always has a funny way of testing even the best of us, doesn't it? Fast forward a few years. After a few massive mistakes and disagreements Earth's Mightiest Heroes find themselves at an impasse.

The death and destruction that seem to always follow these heroes around have stirred the governmental authorities to action. They have resolved to officially clamp down on the team's activities in an effort to avoid further conflict and protect civilian lives. The co-leaders of the Avengers—Captain America and Iron Man—are on the outs. Cap wants to retain the team's autonomy so that they can remain free to fight off any potential threats as they see fit, while Tony has had enough and thinks it's high time that they were all put in check. The rest of the team has to come to terms with the situation and decide which side of the argument they are going to land on.

Meanwhile… a stealthy foe creeps into their lives. He manipulates the facts, uses past errors as leverage and enflames the animosity between the heroes. Soon enough, all-out war breaks out! Hero fights hero; friend fights friend; the team disintegrates [*Captain America: Civil War*, Marvel Studios, 2016].

It's all quite tragic and heartbreaking. How in the world did all of this end up being such an epic mess? Easy answer: these heroes and heroines simply forgot who the real enemy was!

This same scenario plays out so often in our marriages. We build a history together—a history that contains both good and bad, right and wrong, success and failure. Terrible things can happen if we don't remain vigilant and remember that we're in this fight together. We have to IDENTIFY THE REAL ENEMY!

We were in the 18th year of our marriage when we signed those divorce papers. Despite our long history together the enemy was able to infiltrate our front lines and cut off our supply line of trust. It was probably pretty easy for him since we'd already done a lot of the work for him by turning against each other. Satan—the super villain in our story—merely applied pressure to an open wound that was already festering. The painful infection spread, lifelong lovers became mortal enemies and the darkness laughed.

Looking back now, the truth is quite evident to me. Rebecca was never my enemy. The other person in the affair was never my enemy. As much as he'd like me to think otherwise, Satan was—and will always be—the real enemy. Period. Living from that place of clarity allows me to fully forgive, fully trust, fully love.

To avoid any further ambiguity in our relationship, we were committed to fostering an atmosphere of complete transparency. One of the first things we did during our reconciliation was to share all of our device, email and social media passwords with each other. We also decided that we would include each other in text messages with members of the opposite sex.

I remember one time when a male high school friend of Rebecca's started texting her for advice. She quickly added me to the conversation. Her friend was puzzled and asked why that was necessary. Rebecca responded by telling him "We want to protect our marriage at all costs and if there is something you want to share that you're not comfortable letting Scott see then it's something that shouldn't be shared."

Does that seem extreme to you? Maybe. But, uhm, have you read our story?? We haven't put these practices into place from a heart of suspicion or paranoia; we've put them into place from a heart of honor and preservation.

Transparency builds trust, and trust motivates us to circle up back-to-back, swords drawn. From that position we can protect each other, identify the real enemy and quickly mobilize against his attacks.

We are immersed in spiritual warfare; a cosmic battle between good and evil. There was a time when Rebecca and I were in a perpetual state of retreat—stumbling back one misstep away from defeat—but now we are advancing towards the enemy—striding forward together confidently secure in our victory.

We have the power, the passion and the plan. Nothing is going to stop us from winning the battle.

MIND2HEART

In 1513, the dream of creating the Panama Canal was born when the Spanish explorer Vasco Nunez de Balboa crossed the Isthmus of Panama and sighted the Pacific Ocean. The Spanish, Dutch, British and French all tried to create a path between the seas that would shorten the trip from the Atlantic to the Pacific without having to utilize the long and dangerous path around Cape Horn.

Almost 400 years later, on February 1, 1881, the French finally broke ground. Ferdinand de Lesseps, the successful builder of the Suez Canal, estimated that the job would cost $132 million and take 12 years to complete. Unfortunately, the project seemed to be doomed from the beginning. Within the first three years of the project over 600 deaths were recorded. Malaria and yellow fever carried by mosquitos were the most common killers. By 1888, when the French were forced to discontinue their work, $287 million had been spent, a grand total of 11 miles of canal had been dug and twenty thousand men had died. It looked like that this dream would never become reality.

Following the election of 1901, President Theodore Roosevelt rekindled the dream. He emphasized the importance of finishing the canal and urged the U.S. Congress to take swift action.

In 1902, after acquiring the rights to the canal and the leftover equipment from the French for around $40 million—plus the benefit of some questionable behind-closed-doors political wheeling and dealing—the United States continued work on the canal.

On August 15, 1914, the Panama Canal was officially opened. The 50-mile canal cost the U.S. almost $500 million to complete. At the time, it was by far the largest engineering project in American history. That first year 1,000 ships passed through the canal. With German troops on the march in Europe—stoking the flames of World War I—the world barely noticed that after four centuries, the dream had, indeed, become reality [Sources: encyclopedia.com and pbs.org].

It's crazy to think that thousands of men could die, and billions of dollars could be spent working a stretch of land that takes roughly 40 minutes to traverse in a modern-day automobile. But any potential reward requires a measure of risk. Dreams can be costly.

Have you ever heard of the R&S Canal? Don't feel bad if you haven't. It's a small man-made thoroughfare that cuts through Arlington, TX. It sits just north of I-30 only a couple of miles from AT&T Stadium, the home of the Dallas Cowboys.

Construction on the canal was started and finished in the winter of 1991. Like I say, it's pretty tiny. Truth be told, it hasn't really ever served much of a purpose. In fact, before you get frustrated with Google Maps' inability to find it, I need to let you in on a secret… the canal doesn't really exist. It was simply the dream of a young couple that lived in the area at the time. I'll give you a hint. That young couple's initials were "R" and "S" and their pictures have appeared earlier in this book. HashTagObvious.

Rebecca and I had just started dating. I lived in a second-floor apartment with three college buddies. On a crisp November night during a party at my apartment, we both stepped outside and sat at the top of the stairs together. It was the first time we snuggled. Being a diehard romantic, I was obviously inspired by the occasion. I leaned close to her and whispered, "Do you see it?"

Her eyes lifted up to meet mine, "See what?"

"The R & S Canal. It runs right along there." My hand followed the street below us from left to right. I motioned toward the apartment buildings in front of us. "And there are the mountains."

"It's really nice." She giggled.

"And there's the sun." I pointed out the yellow tornado siren peeking out above the rooftops to our right. "The Rebecca and Scott Canal. We can ride it anytime we like. It's ours."

"I love it! I'm so glad it's ours!" Her smile lit up my heart. It was the first time we shared a dream, the first time we got an inkling of what our lives could be like together.

That silly canal crossed my mind as I sat at the top of the third-floor stairwell outside of our family's new apartment. I couldn't help but grin—such a sweet memory. I was hanging out on the steps for a totally different reason these days. In the dead of night, I would slip out of bed, tiptoe down the hallway as not to wake Rebecca and the kids, quietly open the front door and take a seat at the top of the stairs.

I would look out over the apartment complex— thinking, praying, praising and crying. I did lots and lots of crying on those steps. HashTagUglyCry. My hands would get soaked with tears. I would wipe them on my pajama pants and dry my face just in time to start the next round of sobbing.

Losing our home, rebuilding; losing our marriage; rebuilding. The first few months of 2011 had been such a whirlwind. It was like our lives were playing on an old school VCR. Someone was holding down the fast forward button. You could hear the squeals of the tape pushing through the rollers and drums inside the machine as we were frantically jittering around. If we didn't hit the pause button soon, the tape was going to get snagged and it was going to be a bear to get the cassette out intact.

Rebecca and I were functioning under a super high level of stress. For the survival of our marriage and family we had to keep moving forward, but if we didn't manage to TAKE TIME TO HEAL none of it was going to matter.

We had to find healthy ways to mourn what we had lost and process the emotional wounds we had sustained—corporately as a couple and individually as well.

This stairwell had become my fortress of solitude. I don't know how long I sat on those steps every night or how many nights I was out there. I do know that I was constantly sorting through a midnight buffet of emotions. Yeah. Those pesky emotions that I had been shoving down inside of me for so long.

Disappointment, anger and pain took turns streaming down my cheeks. The heat of my face would be cooled by the breeze floating through the stairwell.

It wasn't a place where I found any answers or solved any problems. It was a place where I poured out my heart to God, where I felt the hurt and released it. While these stairwell meetings were an integral part of my healing process, it was also important that I seek out community with others.

When we get overwhelmed by stress or emotion, we can easily isolate ourselves, and that can snowball into other problems like detachment or depression. I knew that was a pit I didn't want to fall into. The Reverend Smokin' Joe Frazier invited me to join a group of guys who met regularly for a Bible study.

It was a group that also included The Longhorn. Since at least a couple of the guys knew my story, I could be comfortable sharing anything I needed to share. We met once a month at a local eatery. We would eat breakfast, discuss Scripture, talk about life and pray for each other. It was a safe place to work through my emotions, seek advice and find answers.

Rebecca had her own group of friends that rallied around her and ministered to her during this time as well. Cultivating friendships is so critical. Having a solid group of believers around us is invaluable as we encounter the tough stuff life throws at us. We wouldn't have made it without our community of faith. There's no question about that.

From the outset, Rebecca had let me know that I could ask her any question about the affair. She was an open book. I just had to decide how much of that book I wanted to read.

I remember talking about it with Dell. He said that based on his personality he would want to know everything so that his mind wouldn't dream up scenarios that didn't really happen. But there wasn't a right or wrong answer. It was all about how much I thought I needed to know.

Ultimately, I decided I didn't need to know much about the details. It would weigh me down and haunt my thoughts. I had seen and heard enough on my own. I didn't need to pile on to what I already knew. It wouldn't be healthy for me.

Having a support system was vital but nothing could replace God in the healing process. I had to come to grips with the fact that it was going to take time. In my case, it took about two-and-a-half years for my emotions to completely heal from the consequences of sin and betrayal.

As I took the necessary steps to heal, I had to LEARN TO DISCERN FEELINGS VS. REALITY. As great as my friends were, I couldn't just rely on their opinions and wisdom. I had to rely on the truth of God's Word—I had to see my feelings through the prism of that truth.

"Truth transcends feelings. Truth transcends facts. You can be presented with the facts without getting the truth. Textbooks can give the facts all day long without necessarily touching on the truth. And, put simply, truth is what God has to say about the facts."
TONY EVANS

I had thoughts and emotions flowing through me that could potentially short-circuit our reconciliation efforts and keep me from fully experiencing God. Did I really believe that Jesus could free me from the pain I was experiencing?

Feelings are real—and God-given—but how could I experience my emotions without being controlled or consumed by them? I decided to take myself through a simple progression of thought that's illustrated by this simple visual...

Whenever I experienced any negative feelings of the moment—sadness, depression, anger, numbness, rage, hopelessness, selfishness, isolation, self-pity, pride, control—I would take an action that moved me toward God—prayer, Bible study, worship, service, thanksgiving—and that would bring me back to the reality of who God is—love, truth, joy, hope, mercy, faithful, peaceful, unchanging, omnipotent, comforter, pure, just.

When emotions would hit me, I would literally sit down, draw this illustration and make a list under each column. I was choosing to base my life on the reality of who God is instead of the feelings I was experiencing. After comparing my feelings and circumstances to God's reality I couldn't help but know that Jesus could free me from the emotions I was feeling.

Within that freedom I was able to allow what I knew about God in my mind to filter down and change my heart; I was able to feel some big nasty emotions, legitimately process them in a healthy way and allow God to completely heal them as only He could; I was able to completely forgive Rebecca and renew our relationship; I was able to pray for those who had hurt me without my feelings getting in the way or skewing my motivations; I was able to let go of any right to get back at anyone for anything that had happened; I was able to let go of the past and focus on the future.

There were still moments where I wanted to throw in the towel. I would get lost in my head trying to figure out why the affair had happened. No matter how hard I pondered it or how many angles I looked at it from none of it made any sense. Why would a friend do such a thing? Was that person ever really my friend? In a Google world where we're used to getting the answer with a twitch of our thumbs, it's hard to reconcile that the answers to those questions just aren't out there.

Swirling emotions of anger and hurt would rise up inside of me as I tried to figure things out. The weight would be too much and I'd just want to get out from under the load. In those moments, I'd ask the Holy Spirit to help me look past my emotions and see God's plan. There was one night when I remember responding to a powerful wave of emotions with a declarative whisper, "This is good, and this is right."

Rebecca and I had dreamed the dream of "R&S Canal" so many years ago. We'd shared a glimpse of what our future might be like together; we'd dared to risk everything as we set our own our journey; we'd faced hardships and obstacles that, at times, seemed overwhelming; we'd accumulated the battle scars that come with being on the frontlines. After taking the time to heal and learning to discern feelings versus reality, we'd given ourselves the chance to once again live together, love together and dream together. Dreams can be costly. But, in the hands of God, the risk will always pale in comparison to the reward.

"Finally, brothers and sisters, whatever is true, whatever is noble, whatever is right, whatever is pure, whatever is lovely, whatever is admirable—if anything is excellent or praiseworthy—think about such things. Whatever you have learned or received or heard from me, or seen in me—put it into practice. And the God of peace will be with you." PHILIPPIANS 4:8-9

WHY2WHAT

We'd made the necessary transition to our new apartment but really didn't have a clue as to where to go from there. Within a couple of weeks, God put it into our minds to check out a town 20 minutes due west. Burleson, Texas—a landlocked town just south of Fort Worth that was famous for being the hometown of Kelly Clarkson. It had a Chili's, Best Buy, and an Academy Sports. What else do you really need?

Rebecca and I toured the area a couple of times and decided that we would try to make the move. It was late May and we wanted to settle in quickly so the boys could have the summer to get acclimated before school started up in the fall. In no time flat we found a house for lease, we applied for it and we were approved. Just like that, we were on the road again!

For a four-month period we were somehow able to pay a mortgage on the previous house, finish out the lease on the apartment and pay the lease payments on the new house. Not sure how that free cash flow worked itself out other than to say God is sovereign.

I guess I needed to have some type of closure, so before we moved out of town, I decided to make one last trip to our old home. I rolled into the cul-de-sac and there it stood—empty and lifeless. As I pressed down on the door handle it sounded like the whole structure let out a deep sigh. Stale grimy air stirred around me as I leaned against the wall in the front room. I slid down into a crouch and dropped my head in prayer.

It felt dark and heavy. As I stared at the black mold growing on the wall across from me, I thanked God for His provision. It was obvious that we had gotten out of there just in time. Within weeks of our move, the place was already uninhabitable.

I walked around the property looking for anything of value we might have forgotten. Nothing was found. I made it back through the house and closed the front door tightly behind me. The building shuddered with an echo of finality. I walked up the path to my car and never looked back.

This old house would become a training ground for the local SWAT team for a few weeks. Soon after that it was unceremoniously knocked down, hauled off piece by piece and, when the dust settled, it was all gone.

I was dealing with the ramifications of what had been done to me. Trust me, that felt like a full-time job. But, at the same time, I had to address the consequences of what I had done. A lifestyle of over-drinking and sexual deviance had wreaked havoc on the lives of the people I cared for the most. My sick cavalier attitude had inflicted damage to my marriage and affected the young women that I'd encountered outside of my covenant relationship.

I had been mired in a sordid world of sexual addiction before God chose to take away that burden in an instant. That was a miracle for sure. But, in reality, it only gave me a running start. I had to decide how I was going to run the race that stretched out ahead of me.

Honestly, it's hard to put myself back in the dark place I was in—to be in a mindset where I thought it was okay to treat women like sexual objects simply made available for my pleasure and satisfaction.

It literally boggles my mind that the Holy Spirit has cleaned me up so thoroughly from the inside out. I'm definitely thankful for the healing and renewal He has given me.

"He lifted me out of the slimy pit, out of the mud and mire; He set my feet on a rock and gave me a firm place to stand." PSALM 40:2

But, I can never forget where I came from. Those memories act as a personal warning to stay sober and sexually pure as well as a public springboard for me to help other people climb out of the pit as well.

If you've convinced yourself that your pornography addiction isn't hurting anyone else but you then you're dead wrong. The sexual attitudes you're establishing influence how you interact with your family, friends and local community. The ripples don't stop there. The pornography industry feeds directly into the global sex trafficking trade.

According to the International Labour Organization there are more than 40 million victims of human trafficking globally. 71% are women and girls [Source: enditmovement.com]. This isn't something that's just happening on the other side of the planet. It's happening in your own backyard. It's estimated that 1.5 million people in the United States are victims of trafficking—mostly for sexual exploitation—and children make up a majority of that number [Source: Reuters].

Unfortunately, Super Bowl weekend has become a powerful magnet for sex trafficking. The millions of party-minded football fans that flock to the event's host cities are targeted by sex traffickers. In 2017, U.S. police arrested 750 people in nationwide sex-trafficking sting operations in the days leading up to the event [Reuters]. At the 2019 Super Bowl in Atlanta federal agents arrested 33 people and rescued 4 human trafficking survivors [enditmovement.com]. Sexual exploitation is a massive epidemic that we need to confront on a personal, national and international level. Check out enditmovement.com for more resources and to see how you can help in this global fight for freedom!

Right now, you might be saying to yourself, "Whoa! Come on now! You've gone too far! You're being ridiculous! I would NEVER be involved in something like that!"

Yeah. And I never thought I would solicit a prostitute either—not once but twice. Remember? Sexual sin is like a Fruit Roll-Up. You get a taste of the excitement and it ramps up from there. Your cravings escalate until, pretty soon, you're embroiled in behavior that you could've never imagined.

When pornography infected my life, I knew what I should do... to put it bluntly... I just needed to STOP it! But that's easier said than done. It can become a vicious cycle. Fail, repent, succeed, fail, repent, succeed, fail... You get the idea.

I ran on the chaotic treadmill of sin prevention for way too long before I was set free. I never want to go there again! How can I guarantee that I won't? I simply need to KNOW THE WHY TO DO THE WHAT!

It's easy to know WHAT we should do. It takes us to a whole new level when we know WHY we should do it!

DIY [Do It Yourself] is big business! In a 2017 market study Technavio predicted that the DIY market will be worth more than $13.9 billion by

2021 [Source: Inc.com]! This incredible surge is being driven by the rise of Google, social media, YouTube and the need for every American male and female to grunt approvingly after a job well done. You can find a Home Depot or Lowe's on every corner these days. It's even intoxicating for a non-handyman like myself. I love the smell of lumber in the morning as I walk into my local Home Depot—delusions of grandeur dancing in my head! To put it in sports terms that I understand better… It's like the beginning of baseball spring training… no matter how bad your team was last year, anything feels possible! "You can do it!"

Just a few weeks ago our dishwasher mysteriously stopped working. Rebecca—a master Googler and expert YouTube hunter—didn't flinch. She glanced at the rogue appliance with disdain and picked up her phone. She searched the make and model of the washer, scrolled through a page or two of queries, fast-forwarded through a few YouTube videos and, just like that, we were ready to open up the patient!

We gathered our random collection of tools and started to pull things apart with bravado! After 5-10 minutes of intense exploratory surgery we were confident that we'd discovered the problem. The little plastic latchy thingy deal—sorry for all of the technical jargon—wasn't working properly. The tip had worn away from overuse and that made it impossible for the door to stay closed and, as a result, the motor wouldn't run.

We ordered the part on Amazon and left the gutted dishwasher disassembled as a warning to our other major appliances to watch themselves. We weren't playing around so don't even think about going on the fritz!

We had to wait 3-5 business days for the new latchy thingy deal to arrive. We can definitely empathize with Ralphie from *A Christmas Story* [1983, MGM] as he waited for his Red Ryder Carbine Action 200-shot Range Model air rifle! It was hard to sleep! It was even harder to stay focused during the day. Would the day EVER come?!? We daydreamed about how satisfying it was going to be to close that dishwasher door and feel that baby purr like a kitten again! We checked our order every hour or so.

"The order's been received!"
"It's been shipped!"
"It's out for delivery!"

Finally, "Christmas Day in July" arrived! I ran outside in my pjs to find a tiny package stuffed in our mailbox! As I triumphantly entered the kitchen doing the cabbage patch, I found Rebecca hunkered down next to the dishwasher ready to receive the part. In one motion I ripped open the padded envelope, caught the part as it hovered in the air and delivered a perfect no-look pass to my Bride!

She caught it and put in place like a pit crew slamming home a new tire. Our adrenaline was running full throttle as we turned on our iPhone flashlights so we could see the screws—our eyes aren't as young as they used to be—and we frantically went to work!

Moments later the patient was completely sewn up and ready to go! Rebecca pulled the latch, the lock engaged, and water started filling the inside of the washer! SUCCESS!!

Euphoria sent us into overdrive! We bumped chests, high-fived and line danced our way into the living room! We fell onto the couch and let out a victorious sigh! Olympic gold medals? World Series Rings? Drinking out of the Stanley Cup? Pssst! Nothing could match this feeling! We'd reached the pinnacle! The rest of our lives would be all downhill from here!

After the first cycle finished, we gleefully unloaded the dishwasher! Everything was SO beautiful! We took turns bringing each dish up to our faces and caressing them with our cheeks! A symphony of slamming cabinets echoed down the street as we put everything away! With permanent smiles in place, we loaded the next round of dishes into the washer.

I felt so powerful in that moment that I'm pretty sure I shut the door with my mind! Rebecca pulled the latch, the lock engaged, and… and… and… NOTHING!!!

Rebecca opened and closed the door again and swung the latch back and forth several times. Silence. Not even a whir to let us know it was trying. It was dead. A dark cloud formed over us as we dropped to our knees and started taking the door apart again. We looked this way and that, jiggled every wire we could find, pulled the latch in and resettled it in hopes of reviving the patient, to no avail. It was a goner.

Our wills were broken. We crawled over to the dining room table and each found a chair. We laid our heads on the table and tried to exhale all of the air out of our bodies. As I reached maximum deflation Rebecca's voice ricocheted off the table and into my ears. "It's probably going to cost just as much to fix this one as it would to just buy a new one." Begrudgingly, I agreed.

With a bittersweet taste in our mouths, we decided that we should head over to Home Depot and purchase a brand-new dishwasher. As we walked out the door, Rebecca gave our old broken-down appliance one last defiant stare as if to say, "You may have won the battle but we will win the war!"

Do you see what happened? We knew the "what"— we wanted to fix that dishwasher on our own—but we couldn't figure out the "why"—we didn't know enough to figure out why it wouldn't work! We had to swallow our pride, reach out beyond our limited abilities and seek expert help.

How often do we try to fix our own sin? We try to self-regulate the problem. It's doesn't take too long before we realize that we really can't reconcile the dilemma on our own. We need help; we need someone who knows the solution; we need someone who can make us new again.

"For all have sinned and fall short of the glory of God, and all are justified freely by his grace through the redemption that came by Christ Jesus." ROMANS 3:23-24

Jesus knows what we need and why we need it! Remember when He busted into the temple and flipped some tables? The religious leaders had allowed the temple to become corrupted. They were gouging Gentile [non-Jewish] worshippers with crazy high prices and fees. Jesus was letting them know that shouldn't be the normal operating procedure. His house should be a house of prayer! HashTagBoomshakalaka!

What happens right after that is even more powerful! The blind and lame flocked to Him. He healed them so that they could have access to the temple and freely worship [MATTHEW 21:12-16].

He's still doing the same thing for us right here and right now! His sacrifice affords us the opportunity to choose the blessing instead of the curse. There is so much power within the depths of God's goodness!

We can get so easily lost in the minutiae of fixing every little part of ourselves—"God wants me to work on this right now or that right now."—when, in reality, He actually wants to adjust our attitudes about everything all at once. Change can then come from a place of freedom instead of bondage.

I'd like to share three phrases that can help free you from the oppression of sexual sin...

1. YOU ARE FREE. The moment you repent of sin you're freed from it! Don't fall for the lie that you're still tied to your sin. It literally has no hold over you anymore. JOHN 8:36... "So if the Son sets you free, you will be free indeed."

2. YOU CAN SEE IN 3D. The object of your lust— on the screen, on the page, in your mind or right there next to you—is a three-dimensional person with hopes, dreams, fears and sins of his/her own. He/she needs Christ as much as you do. Grasping that reality can morph lust—wanting something

from someone—into love—wanting something for someone.

3. SEX IS NOT A NEED. Remember that sex is not just a physical need. It is an expression of the ultimate intimacy we have with Christ. It's the culmination of the marriage covenant. 1 CORINTHIANS 6:16 [MSG]… "There's more to sex than mere skin on skin. Sex is as much spiritual mystery as physical fact. As written in Scripture, 'The two become one.' Since we want to become spiritually one with the Master, we must not pursue the kind of sex that avoids commitment and intimacy, leaving us more lonely than ever—the kind of sex that can never 'become one.'"

Don't settle for the surface level thrill. Dig deeper to find the blessing within God's will.

If your heart is changing then your behavior will change right along with it! Sin will become less and less desirable. You will be able to thrive inside healthy sexual boundaries that feel comforting rather than constraining.

When you realize how much God cares for you, obedience will start to feel less like a chore and more like worship. Submission to God's will allows you to cultivate a more intimate fellowship with the Creator of the universe. Plus, there's no doubt that OBEDIENCE HAS ITS REWARDS!

In January of 2012, I received a call from one of the production companies I work with. They were doing a corporate gig in Barcelona, Spain and wanted to know if I would be interested in helping out. I responded emphatically, "YES! Pick me!" The producer suggested that Rebecca come along too! He didn't have to ask twice—we were all in!

A few days later, I received an email with the event details. I almost fell out of my chair when I read it. The show was scheduled for the middle of April which coincided exactly with the one-year anniversary of our reconciliation! There was no way it could be a coincidence!

The last 300 days had been both gut-wrenching and wonderful as we followed God's lead in rebuilding the framework of our family from the ground up. It had called for a ton of hard work that had resulted in so many blessings already. But, apparently, God wasn't done! He wanted to throw us a shindig halfway across the world! And, believe me, we were ready to party Hardie! Sorry—couldn't resist that pun. HashTagSmileyFace.

Rebecca and I touched down in Barcelona a week before my work was set to commence. We walked the famous Los Rambles, immersed ourselves in the amazing La Boqueria Market, marveled at the creativity of the Museo Picasso and Sagrada Familia Cathedral, and indulged our appetites at Els Quatre Gats—Picasso's old hangout!

I'll never forget the moment when we strolled hand-in-hand across the beach into the gentle tide flowing over the naturally weathered crushed stone. As the waters of the Mediterranean Sea washed over our bare feet, we offered thanksgiving and praise to God! He'd given us such an extravagant gift simply because He loved us!

Knowing the "why" behind God's love has helped us identify what we need to do to safeguard our purity and foster an atmosphere within our home that welcomes His presence.

We don't choose obedience because we want something from Christ. He's already given so much. He truly owes us nothing. We choose obedience because we love Him.

"Anyone who loves me will obey my teaching. My Father will love them, and we will come to them and make our home with them."
JOHN 14:23

OLD2NEW

1986 had its share of over-the-top television programming. There was the one about a smart-mouthed alien who crash-landed in a suburban garage [*ALF*]! What about those two pastel-clad fashion-conscious police detectives Crockett and Tubbs who fought crime with their own custom soundtrack thumping in the background [*Miami Vice*]? "I pity da fool" that never experienced Hannibal, Faceman, B.A. and Murdock blasting their way through the bad guys in that tricked out black and red GMC Vandura cargo van [*The A-Team*]! And, while we're on the subject of cars, who wouldn't want a super-powered, hyper-intelligent, souped-up Pontiac Trans-AM that can drive 300 miles an hour, is bulletproof, fireproof and can talk [*Knight Rider*]?!?

As mind-bending as those shows were there's nothing that prepared the unsuspecting public for the pièce de résistance Geraldo Rivera unleashed on

April 21, 1986… *The Mystery of Al Capone's Vaults*!

Al Capone was the head of organized crime in Chicago during the 1920s. His organization called the "Chicago Outfit" generated $100 million in revenue annually and employed more than 600 gangsters throughout Chicago. The business model included: racketeering, prostitution, burglary, drug trafficking, money laundering, bootlegging, gambling, extortion and murder. Yep—lots of good times, I'm sure!

Al set up his headquarters in the 10-story Lexington Hotel on the south side of Chicago. Capone and his cronies occupied the second, fourth and fifth floors. Tommy-gun-toting bodyguards were posted throughout the premises. The building was fashioned with secret staircases and underground tunnels that made for an easy getaway if the authorities or rival crime bosses came calling [Source: myalcaponemuseum.com].

At the height of his powers, Scarface—the nickname the press gave him which, by the way, he hated—was estimated to be worth $1.3 billion!

In 1931, after years of failed attempts, Al was finally arrested for tax evasion. He was sentenced to 11 years and ended up in the maximum-security federal prison on Alcatraz Island. Capone contracted neurosyphilis early in his sentence and became so debilitated that he was released after eight years of incarceration. He lived out the rest of his days with his wife and grandkids in a mansion in Miami where he died of a stroke in 1947.

He left behind a huge mystery. Where in the world had all of his money gone?! Legend had it that large sums of loot had been tucked away in the catacombs of the Lexington Hotel.

Enter stage left Geraldo Rivera, a once promising investigative reporter whose career had stalled out after being fired from ABC News. He was on the lookout for something to jumpstart his career. So, when freelance producers came to him with the idea to excavate Capone's former lair on live TV—plus the appropriate amount of monetary compensation—he jumped at the chance.

30 million viewers tuned in to watch the primetime excavation of the Lexington Hotel. I was one of them—the whole endeavor caught my imagination. It was like a modern-day treasure hunt! I was glued to my TV screen.

For two hours, Geraldo shouted over power tools, ignited dynamite and teased the possibility of finding money, weapons or the dead bodies of Capone's former enemies [Sources: mentalfloss.com and thevintagenews.com].

After using the rudimentary sonogram equipment of the time, they discovered what appeared to be a hollow space in the basement of the hotel. Did it contain Scarface's lost treasure? There was a 22-inch-thick wall of concrete and brick covering up a potentially historic find!

15 minutes into the broadcast, a Bobcat was chained up to the concrete slab and on Geraldo's "Go!" it accelerated. The wall came crashing down! For a moment the screen was filled with a puff of smoke. I was on the edge of my floral-themed sofa! What could it be?!? Skeletons? Gold bars? Mounds of antiquated cash? Rivera's colossal mustache emerged from behind the veil of dust.

"Welp. So far it's just '20's junk!" The tips of his mustache hung low as he lifted up an empty bottle. "Come on! Let's clean this out! Let's go!"

A crew of workers started shoveling mounds of dirt out of the chamber. After another hour and 45 minutes, they'd only dug up a few empty bottles, copious amounts of debris and, of all things, a stop sign. Geraldo was now faced with a sobering realization... there was absolutely nothing of value in the vault.

Rivera was devastated. He thanked all of the workers and staggered off camera into the shadows.

Right after the broadcast, Geraldo locked himself in his hotel room, took the phone off the hook and got "tequila drunk." It's still known as one of the most profound failures in the history of live television! Not quite the career rebirth he'd imagined!

With every careless word that we spoke—with every moment we chose selfishness over servanthood—Rebecca and I were building a wall. In the end, a sturdy barrier of relational apathy stood between us and the treasure of true Godly intimacy.

As the wall grew taller the trash filled up every open space. I couldn't see her clearly and I had no idea what was going on inside of her heart. Despite the circumstances I had hope that there was still something of great value just waiting to be unearthed. I knew I didn't have the power to seize it on my own. It was well above my pay grade.

Out of nowhere—in the darkest of nights—God made Himself known. Within the grip of His

fierce love the wall between us was ripped
down. In a heartbeat, we could see each other
again; impurity and pride were instantly
replaced with innocence and humility.

We could experience the treasure of each other once
again! That was remarkable! But that didn't mean
there wasn't a ton of work ahead of us. Cleaning out
the mountain of rubbish that had accumulated
behind our wall was going to take time, patience
and tenacity.

From the moment that Rebecca and I embraced in
the kitchen—with our boys whooping and hollering
around us—everything felt so fresh! We knew that
we never wanted to stagger off into the shadows
again!

Like Geraldo, we'd experienced a public failure of
gigantic proportions. Going off the grid and hiding
out wasn't an option for us. We weren't going to
waste this opportunity. God's glory was at stake and
our personal reputations paled in comparison. No

matter what might lie ahead of us we weren't going to shirk our responsibility to own our mistakes and accept the consequences.

Unlike Geraldo, we weren't surprised by the gunk we found when the wall came down. Some of our friendships were never going to be the same. We'd hurt a lot of people with our actions. Friends walked away. I don't begrudge them at all. It's hard when you've been lied to and betrayed. I totally get it.

Those shots to the belly were hard to take, but it didn't knock us down for the count. God used each hit to reinforce our humility and strengthen our reliance on Him. We were able to stand taller—not for our own glory, but for His glory!

With the wall between us gone we reveled in a renewed intimacy. Even when we were working through hard things and dealing with intense emotions our mantra would be, "DON'T PUT ANOTHER BRICK IN THE WALL!"

We can talk to each other so easily now. We're free to be ourselves in a way that we'd never experienced in our relationship before. It's SO energizing! It's something we never want to lose.

At times our old relational habits will resurface. Defensiveness can get in the way of openness. We can both feel it and we don't like it! HashTagNoBueno.

There was one time in our rental house when we'd been hashing out some tough stuff. Eventually, the conversation took a turn and became heated. Rebecca retreated up the stairs to the second floor. She plopped down on the love seat in the middle of the game room. There I was left at the bottom of the stairs with my hands resting on my hips.

Suddenly, a thought came to my mind: "Ya know, Scooter, this ain't going so good! Ya might want to do something about this…" I dropped my defensive stance and ran up the stairs. She was sitting forward

with her head down and jaw set. She didn't react to
my sudden appearance.

"Hey babe… this feels a lot like the 'old us,'
doesn't it?"

"Yes. Yes, it does."

I sat on the arm of the chair. "We can't let that
happen…"

She turned toward me with desperation in her eyes,
"I know, Scott! We can't let ONE brick go up on
that wall again! We just can't!"

I slid down into the chair next to her and wrapped
my arms around her. "And we won't! Let's pray
and then start this conversation over the right way."

And that's what we did. And that's what we do.
EVERY. TIME. Whenever we have a brick in one
hand and we're slathering mortar in place with the
trowel in our other hand, we stop for a beat. We

recognize what's happening, we put down the brick and we reset.

We cherish our intimacy and we understand the need to protect it! We know that it takes intentionality; it takes humility; it takes submission; it takes servanthood; it takes everything we have. And it's SO worth it!

Keeping that wall down—and nurturing our intimacy with God—doesn't just benefit us on a personal level. It gives us the opportunity to share Christ's love with everyone around us in the marketplace.

Francis Chan nailed it when he said:

"Marriage is such a powerful way to display the Gospel and the glory of God. It is the first place people will look to see if we really believe what we say we believe."

Jesus isn't wearing blinders when He looks at us.

Even though He sees everything—the upright and unpleasant—He chooses to adore us. He wants us to move from who we think we are to who He knows we are. He wants us to be released from the bondage that weighs us down so that we can freely experience the abundance of His love! If we can reflect that type of love in our marriages then the world will take notice and hearts will be changed.

It's pretty cool when you're just doing your thing and God works through you. We're surprised every time someone comes up to us and tells us how our marriage has inspired them in some way. Rebecca and I usually glance at each other with a slight shoulder shrug and give each other a look like, "What'd we do?"

The only way I can really answer that question is to say that we're ALL IN. We're all in on the love of God—a love that has comforted us in deeply personal ways and radically changed our hearts. We're all in on our marriage covenant—a covenant that has deepened our capacity to love no matter the circumstance. We're all in on God's Word—a practical life-giving Word that we live by all day every day.

God is the premiere home builder in the universe! He uses only the finest materials that are made to last! His attention to detail will blow you away! Every room will have a special personal touch— filled with rare and beautiful treasures! Trust me… You'll never ever want to find another home! HashTagTheUltimateHomeOwnersAssociation.

"My people will live in peaceful dwelling places, in secure homes, in undisturbed places of rest." ISAIAH 32:18

This is the story that God has written for us. He stepped into the middle of the tragedy we were writing and took it upon Himself to rewrite it into an epic love story full of grace, redemption and hope.

He has a story ready for you too. Look for His hand. See what He's writing. It definitely won't be a snoozer! It'll be a tale that keeps you on the edge of your seat! There'll be valleys that you could never imagine climbing out of and mountain tops so high that it will take your breath away.

It'll have all the elements that make up any great best seller—heroes, villains, pain, loss, adventure and victory!

So be bold. Choose to love. Choose to forgive. Choose to serve. Choose to endure. When we willingly put all that we are into God's hands He will forge something that is beautiful and priceless! God will lift you up and the shine will be so bright that the darkness will be subdued. You will become a Trophy of God's Grace!

EPILOGUE

After three years of living in rental properties—actually two houses in the same neighborhood—we were able to become homeowners again. PTL!

We've been in our current home since 2015. There's a two-sided wooden sign hanging right next to our front door. One side says, "Hardies: est. 1992" and the other side says, "Please come in!" When that sign is out—which happens more often than not—there's no need to knock!

Our friends and family are always welcome to just bust on in! We live in a vibrant place with tons of hustle and bustle. There's lots of life being lived here! We hope and pray that people will always find solace and comfort in our home—that Christ's light is always shining brightly!

While we're always willing to go wherever He wants whenever he wants, we're so thankful for the chance to live, worship and build community here. HashTagHomeIsWhereTheHeartIs.

Not too long ago we were invited to an 18th Birthday/Graduation party at Randol Mill Park in Arlington. That just so happens to be where we were married! Ironically enough it was around the same time as our 25th Wedding Anniversary!

On our way to the party we decided that once we got to the park, we would drive over to the softball field where we tied the knot. We were really excited about walking the field and reliving our special day! As we parked outside the left field fence—right where the limo had made its entrance onto the field so many seasons ago—we noticed that a Little League baseball game was being played.

That kinda ruined our plans but we figured we'd walk up and check it out anyway. We stood by the third base dugout and watched a half inning of the game. As both teams converged on their respective dugouts, I had a crazy idea. I walked over to one of the coaches and introduced myself.

"Hey! I know this is odd but my Bride and I were married on this field 25 years ago. We were wondering if it would be too much to ask for us to run out to the pitcher's mound and take a quick selfie."

The coach did a double take and then said, "Sure. Let me check." He trotted over to talk to the other coaches and umpires. After a quick huddle they turned around and motioned for us to enter the field.

We snaked our way through the dugout, onto the infield and planted our feet firmly on the pitching rubber. We made the necessary adjustments so that we could see home plate in the background behind us. I lifted my phone high in the air, we grinned from ear to ear and I snapped the picture.

I'll never forget what happened as we stepped away from the mound. I heard a murmur going through the crowd. They were starting to realize that this crazy couple actually had a legitimate reason to have a photo shoot right in the middle of their game!

Suddenly all of the parents, players, coaches and umpires burst into applause! It was crazy! We were getting a standing ovation! I tipped my cap in appreciation and Rebecca waved as vigorously as she could. We high-fived our way through the dugout and then gave our fans one last big wave!

For two lifelong baseball fans like us we couldn't have imagined a bigger moment than that!! We giggled all the way back out to the parking lot!

Lord, thank you for the awesome anniversary gift! You really shouldn't have. ☺

"Every good and perfect gift is from above, coming down from the Father of the heavenly lights, who does not change like shifting shadows." JAMES 1:17

Made in the USA
Coppell, TX
28 December 2020

47241295R00115